THE MUSICIANS

Liam McAuley

iUniverse, Inc.
New York   Bloomington

The Musicians

iUniverse books may be ordered through booksellers or by contacting:

iUniverse
1663 Liberty Drive
Bloomington, IN 47403
www.iuniverse.com
1-800-Authors (1-800-288-4677)

Because of the dynamic nature of the Internet, any Web addresses or links contained in this book may have changed since publication and may no longer be valid. The views expressed in this work are solely those of the author and do not necessarily reflect the views of the publisher, and the publisher hereby disclaims any responsibility for them.

ISBN: 978-1-4502-7607-8 (pbk)
ISBN: 978-1-4502-7609-2 (cloth)
ISBN: 978-1-4502-7608-5 (ebk)

Printed in the United States of America

iUniverse rev. date: 11/18/10

To Goran Blaznic and
Predrag Milicevic,
the Bosnian boys whose
courage inspired me

~ **Contents** ~

~ **Foreword** ~

My friend Liam, the author of this book, asked me to read one of the last printed copies of the first edition. During our conversation, he stated that he is somewhat puzzled as to why his eighty-three-page used paperback book is presently being sold over the Internet for $135–$185. As I read the book, I realized the appeal, and I discovered that it was hard to stop until I reached the very last page. *The Musicians* is easy and enjoyable reading for almost all ages. This book chronicles the adventures and misadventures of two Irish boys in America before and during the Mexican War and before and during the Civil War, as well as their trip as cabin boys on a large cargo sailboat from Belfast to New York. Although the story itself is fiction, it reflects many historical details from American history. In my opinion, as well as the opinion of my wife, Maya, this book is an excellent piece of work and a pleasure to read. I am glad that the author is preparing a second edition, as I will buy the first copy of that book!

Dr. Joseph Stephen Schon
Former professor,
University of New York in Prague and Anglo-American University of Prague, and former director of (National Registry of Environmental Professionals).

~ Out of Ireland ~

It all started on a street in Belfast. I was the typical Irish kid, with black hair and blue eyes and a round face with dimples. It was 1846, and I was only twelve years old, begging for some money. A couple came by. They were all dressed up in fancy clothes, and the missus had plenty of jewelry on. She was also loaded up with that sweet-smelling stuff called perfume. I went up all polite and asked them, "I beg your pardon, miss; could you spare a halfpenny?"

"Harry!" the missus cried. "Get this street urchin away from me!" She continued to scream. I realized that my bruised lip had scared her, rather than bringing out sympathy; I had been in a fight earlier with some Protestant boys.

Harry gave me a push. "Get out of here, you piece of filth," he shouted.

I responded in anger. "Your missus is the one who uses that sweet-smelling stuff to try to hide her stench, not me," I told him.

Harry raised his hand to swing at me, but I ducked it and ran around the missus a few times as she screamed. Harry was still trying to catch me, so I decided to get out of there before a constable came.

As I ran down the street, I heard someone call my name: "Ian, Ian!"

I turned around and saw my friend Danny Higgins.

"Ian, your lip … you got into another fight with the Protestant boys, didn't you?"

"Aye, it took four of them to get me down," I told him. "I landed a few good hits on them before they knocked me down." I could tell immediately that he wasn't really interested in the story of my fight. He was hopping from foot to foot and excitedly waving a newspaper in the air.

"There is a story about America in the paper. Will you read it to me?" he asked.

Danny had grand thoughts about America and dreamed of going there. He was only eleven; his mother had died when he was very young, and his father was too drunk to care about him. He spent most of his time with me, on the streets, and I took care of him.

"Okay, Danny, let me see the paper," I told him, and he handed it to me. "They're talking about building a railroad from the East Coast of the United States to the West Coast—a place called California."

"Isn't California where the lost cities of gold are?"

"Yeah," I said, "there are seven of them. The Indians hid them from the Spanish." I knew what he was leading up to: going to California and searching for the cities of gold.

Sure enough, he said, "Ian, we could go there and look for them. I was down at the docks and saw all these ships getting ready to leave for America. I asked a sailor, and he said they were going to New York, where we could take the train to California."

"We could, Danny, but I don't think the trains will be running for a while."

"You could get us on a ship going to America, Ian."

He had much more faith in me than I did. I did not know how I was going to pull it off, but I said to him anyway, "Let's go see the ships, Danny."

"All right, Ian ... but first let me play a new drumbeat that I heard the British soldiers marching to." He pulled out two sticks that he had whittled to resemble drumsticks and began rapping them against the side of a building. He loved the sound of drums and would follow the British soldiers around just to hear them. With his two sticks, he would try to imitate the drumbeats he had heard. I don't know how he did it, but it sounded good.

"What do you think, Ian?"

"It is good, Danny, but the ships are waiting."

We set off for the docks.

Everything was just as Danny had described. I had never seen the docks so busy; ships were being loaded up everywhere we looked. But what amazed me most was the cargo. They were packing people into the ships like cattle. I figured at this rate, Ireland would be empty by Christmas. Maybe Danny was right; maybe it was time to leave.

"See, Ian? All these ships are going to America."

"Aye, I do believe you are right."

Looking around, I saw a sailor coming up from the docks and stopped him to explore the possibilities. "Excuse me, sir."

"What is it, son? I'm in a hurry," he said gruffly.

"Me and my friend wanted to become cabin boys; we are hard workers. Do you know a ship that might need some?"

"Can't help you, son. Like I said, I'm in a hurry."

He started to walk away, but I stepped in front of him. "Please, sir."

"You are a persistent little bastard."

"A bastard? Oh, no, sir. I know *who* my mother and father are, and they were married. It's just that I do not know *where* they are."

He softened a little at this and said, "An educated one, too. All right, I just might know of one. It's called the *Courageous*, and its captain is Old Jim Stewart. We're heading out for New York in the morning. It's a lot of work, and the conditions will be harsh. You still interested?"

Before I could say anything, Danny answered. "Yes, sir, we are! I am Danny Higgins, and he is me friend Ian Walsh."

A friendly grin came over the sailor's face, and then he laughed. "Okay, then go down to that ship there." He pointed to a ship on the dock. "Tell Old Jim that John Moore sent you. I'll meet you there later, after I run a few errands. Now off with you."

I thought for a minute. There was one more thing to take care of.

"Sir, how much will we be paid?"

He started laughing and shaking his head.

"One American dollar," he responded.

"We will need two, sir," I answered back with confidence.

"You're a shrewd lad. I'll give you two if I see you work hard."

"Yes, sir, we will."

"Now go!"

We ran down to the ship. Standing on deck with his back to us was a tall, thin man.

I yelled, "Yo, on board! I am looking for Captain Stewart."

The man on deck turned around to see who had spoken. His face looked like the bottom of my shoe—worn, dirty—and under his nose was a gray, waxed handlebar mustache that was slightly off center. "You found him. So speak your mind; I've got work to do."

"Mr. Moore sent us," I answered. "He said you were looking for some cabin boys."

"Well, I'm not, but Mr. Moore must be if he sent you here. I knew he would find some way out of the kitchen duties I gave him. Well, just wait there 'til he comes back. What will he think of next?"

We sat down on the dock and waited. Sailors began arriving at the boat and started work. I could hear Old Jim hollering instructions to the men as they set to their tasks. Singing commenced, and the sails came out, ready to be hoisted up when the captain gave the command.

Old Jim hollered to us from the deck, "Boys, himself is coming."

I looked up and saw Mr. Moore coming down the ramp to the dock. He winked at us and went on board, where he talked to Old Jim. A few minutes later, he motioned to us to come aboard, also.

Once on board, we were introduced to the crew and then taken to the kitchen, where we met the cook, Jack. "Fellows, this is where you will spend most of the journey to New York, so get used to it," Mr. Moore told us. "Jack here will tell you what to do. Don't let me down. I went out on a limb for you with Old Jim, and it will be my butt if you mess up."

Jack, the cook, started us working right off. The ship suffered no shortage of pots to be secured, food to put away, and floorboards to be scrubbed. We heard many jokes from Jack. Most were not worth repeating, but he seemed to enjoy them. Time passed quickly, and nightfall arrived.

Mr. Moore came down to tell us about the next day. He always started off by calling us fellows. "Fellows, we leave at eight in the morning; I want you here at six. Now, go get yourselves some rest, because tomorrow is a big day."

As I walked away from the dock, heading toward the Falls section of town, it hit me. I was sailing to *America* the next day.

I arrived at six the next morning. Danny was already there, waiting. I had spent the night alone, thinking I might change my mind, but I knew what I had to do.

Danny greeted me. "Ian, Mr. Moore has breakfast for you down below. I already ate with the crew. When you are done, we clean up and get ready for the lunch."

I went below, ate, and talked to Jack—though Jack did all the talking—and then we cleaned up. Up on top, the crew was getting ready to set sail. The ship was nearly loaded with its cargo, clothing for New York. Danny went on deck to watch the send-off, but I stayed below. Work remained to be done in the kitchen, and I did not really want to say good-bye to Ireland.

The trip had gotten off to a good start, and I was starting to enjoy sailing. My favorite spot was at the bow of the ship, looking out over the blue ocean that never seemed to end. Here was where I did most of my writing in the diary Mr. Moore had given me earlier, along with my very own pen. He thought I might want to record my adventures while aboard the ship. Old Jim was good enough to give me ink. He never spoke much, but he seemed to know his crew inside out.

I had learned to read and write from my parish priest, Father Thomas Kelly. Every Sunday after Mass, he would take us kids and give us lessons. I always remember what he said to us: "The knowledge to read and write will open doors that you could never imagine. New worlds will be at your disposal." My father would laugh at me when I would read him a story. He thought I was wasting my time and energy, but it did not discourage me. I stuck with it and learned as much as I could from Father Kelly. That is why Danny always asked me to read to him.

Danny was having a great time. I had never seen him so happy. He always had a smile on, and the crew nicknamed him "Smiles." Mr. Moore did a good job looking after us. He showed me what sailing was all about and gave me my own watch on deck. We slept in what they called hammocks. It was a piece of canvas tied to a pole at each end. It wrapped around to hold you in. The ship could rock all it wanted, and you wouldn't know it. It was better than sleeping on the streets.

The navigator on board went by the name of Billy, and he, along with Old Jim, was responsible for keeping the ship on course.

I tried to learn as much as I could. The trip to New York would take us about twenty-three days by Billy's calculations, and they passed without much excitement.

We were about four days away from New York when a storm hit us. At first, I could not believe the size of the waves. I watched from the bow of the ship until the wind and rain picked up and made it impossible to stay there. Old Jim ordered that the sails be taken down. The crew came together and had them down and tied in less than twenty minutes, and I helped. Everyone started heading in to wait out the storm, and on my way in, out of nowhere, a tremendous wall of water appeared. I stood motionless. Next it came crashing down on me with such force, I found myself being thrown about. I had managed to grab hold of some rigging and found myself dangling in it off the side of the ship. Mr. Moore slid himself down along the deck and grabbed hold of my hand.

"Ian, take your other hand and grab on tight to my arm."

"I can't! My hand is wrapped up in some rope! I can't get it free," I yelled over the sound of the wind.

Billy slid down along the side of Mr. Moore. "Don't worry, chap, I'll have you free in just a few seconds." He pulled out his knife and cut the rope that was holding my hand.

I grabbed Mr. Moore's arm as he pulled me up and said, "All right, fellow, let's get below."

I met Danny down below, which is where he had been from the beginning of the storm. "Ian, you are all white," Danny observed. "What happened? You see a monster?"

Billy and Mr. Moore began to laugh.

"No, not exactly," I told him, thinking fast. I had to make this sound good, so I said, "A huge hand reached on deck, grabbed me around the ankle, and started to pull me into the sea. I grabbed onto some rigging and held on for my life. Then Mr. Moore and Billy came and pulled me in."

Mr. Moore broke up my story by saying, "I thought you were going to swim to New York and beat us there."

Billy, who was really laughing now, added, "I think you've been hanging around Jack too much."

Well, I had survived. I found a place to lie down and fell asleep. There was a calm all around. It felt good until I found myself in the air and then back down on the wooden floor after a hard landing, looking up at Old Jim. He had a stern look on his face as he stared down at me.

"Get up! Get up! I'm not paying you to sleep!" he shouted down at me.

I jumped to my feet and stuttered, "Y-yes, sir!"

"Get down below and help Jack," he ordered. I ran.

Down below, Jack had already put my food out. I sat down to eat, and Jack sat down right next to me. I knew I was in for a story.

"Did I ever tell you about the time I was on the HMS *Victory*?" he asked.

He did not wait for me to reply. Jack had told me this story many times, but he needed to tell it again. He seemed to live in his tales, and for a few moments, he could go anywhere or be anything he wanted. He started his retelling, and I sat there and listened.

"Well, we were off the coast of France. A storm had separated us from the rest of the fleet. Three French ships had spotted us and started to close in. The captain was sure we would be sunk, but he hoped to be able to take one, maybe two, with us. I went up to the captain and told him I had an idea that just might work, and he liked it. So I made up this stew in a big iron pot I brought up from the kitchen, placed it at the stern of the ship, and lit it on fire. The thickest black smoke came out from the pot and covered the air so that you could not see a thing. The wind took it in the direction of the French ships. We lost sight of the three ships in the smoke and headed as fast as the wind would take us back to England."

"You saved the day, huh, Jack?"

"Sure did—received a medal from the king himself." He pulled out a medal from his pocket and showed it to me. The prized medal was extremely worn, and no markings could be made out, but to Jack, it had come from the king.

"Well, Jack, should we get ready for chow?"

Just then, Danny came down. "Ian, tomorrow morning we should be sailing into New York, and Mr. Moore said I could have the lookout in the crow's nest. I'll be the first one to spot land."

He had such a gleam of joy and peace in his eyes. A dream was about to come true for him; he would be stepping off the ship onto American soil.

I did not know what waited for us on that soil, but that did not seem to matter. "That's great, Danny. Just make sure you don't miss it."

"Not a chance. Are we ready for chow?"

"Almost. Why don't you give us a hand?" I suggested.

"Sure. Oh, Mr. Moore said not to forget the monkey's blood."

"The what?" I was puzzled, as I did not know what "monkey's blood" was.

Jack interrupted. "I'll take care of the monkey's blood. Tell Mr. Moore not to worry."

I still did not know what they were talking about, so I said, "Okay, Jack, but what is it?"

A smile appeared on his face. "Red wine. It is a tradition on our last night at sea. I've got French monkey's blood for tonight."

We had our last dinner, and I tasted monkey's blood for the first time. I did enjoy it; the glass that I had was small, but it was enough for me to appreciate its full value.

I finished my chores after dinner and went up on deck to my favorite spot on the bow. The sun had gone down, but plenty of stars were out, and I started writing by starlight. Mr. Moore sat down next to me, and we just talked about everything.

"Ian, I hope you don't mind my letting Danny go up in the crow's nest tomorrow," he said at one point.

"No," I told him. "It means a lot to him, and it was nice of you to do that for him. He was so excited about it that I don't think he will get much sleep tonight."

"I don't know, but I believe the monkey's blood took care of that. He is sound asleep below—he did not even make it to his bunk."

"What'd Old Jim say?"

"He doesn't know."

"That's good," I said, relieved that the captain wasn't aware of Danny's intoxication.

I had a question for Mr. Moore. "I have been meaning to ask you. Why does Old Jim wear his mustache under his right nostril like that?"

"I don't know, and I'm not going to ask him. You better not, either."

"What makes you think I would ask him?"

"I know you. You have that look in your eyes. When you want to know something, nothing stops you."

I chuckled and said, "Yeah, I'll find out before we get to New York."

Mr. Moore yawned. "Well, fellow, I think it is getting late, and you should turn in for some shut-eye. I see you are writing in your diary."

"Yes, sir—I want to thank you for it. And I think I will turn in now."

I had gotten up to head down below, when Mr. Moore called to me, "Oh, Ian, did you ever hear the story of how curiosity killed the cat?"

"No, sir, I don't think so?"

"I will have to tell it to you sometime."

"Yes, sir," I uttered with a smirk.

"Good night, fellow," he said.

It was obvious I had him worried. He did not know what I might do to find out the secret of Old Jim's mustache. There was no need for him to worry, though. I had everything under control. I went down below to my bunk, and before I could get both my shoes off, I was asleep.

Mr. Moore woke both me and Danny up early the next day. "Let's go, fellows. Time is wasting and stops for no man."

Danny was a little slow to get up, and Mr. Moore looked at him and grinned. Then he went back up on deck.

I looked at Danny; he was moving, but very slowly.

"What's the matter?" I asked.

"My head, Ian … I think it grew overnight. It feels funny."

"You just need some fresh air. So hurry on up there; New York is waiting," I said, trying to rouse him.

"Oh, yeah! I will let you know when I can see it."

"Good—just make sure you don't miss it."

Danny moved quickly now and, on his way up on deck, shouted back to me, "Not a chance, Ian."

I had my own chores to do. Jack was waiting for me in the kitchen. I went straight to work. Jack, I noticed, was getting Old Jim's breakfast ready.

"Jack, I will take Old Jim's breakfast to him. Danny is up on top, in the crow's nest."

"Yes, why don't you?" he replied. "Make sure you knock before you go in."

"I will, Jack."

Up the steps leading to the captain's chambers I went. I stopped outside the door, which was ajar just enough for me to see in. If Old Jim were going to shave, it would be this morning, before we docked in New York. Jack had said to make sure to knock, so I would … after I took a look inside. Everything was just as I had expected. Old Jim had a pan of water, shaving cream on his face, and a razor in his right hand. It looked as if everything was normal, and then he reached the mustache. I watched very carefully. Suddenly, the ship made a move that caused Old Jim to slip, and off came half the mustache.

"Those bloody fools—they did it to me again!"

It was hard, but I held in my laugh for fear of my life. It now was the right time to knock, so I got up the courage and rapped on the door.

"What do you want?" Old Jim asked crossly.

"It is Ian, sir; I have your breakfast."

"Just put it on my desk and get out of here," he growled, and that is just what I did.

Jack and I got the rest of the chow ready for the crew. Danny stayed up in the crow's nest. I put some food away for him and Billy, who stayed up there with him. Mr. Moore looked across the table at me. I gave him a smile, and he just shook his head.

Up on deck, Danny started yelling. "Land ho! Land ho! New York is off the starboard bow."

I ran up on deck to see. It was faint, but I could make out land in the distance.

"Well, Ian, there it is: America," said Mr. Moore. "It won't be long now."

"Yes, sir. It's beautiful."

"Do you know what you are going to do yet?" he asked.

"No. Just look around, I guess."

"There's plenty to see. I have to go see the captain; I will talk to you later about the mustache." He winked at me and headed for the captain's chambers, but he never did ask me about it. I guess he liked the secrecy of not knowing.

Late that afternoon, the *Courageous* docked in New York's harbor. Danny and I were getting our belongings together—not that there was much to gather—when Mr. Moore called down to us. "Fellows, the captain wants to see you before you go ashore."

Thoughts started to go through my head, and then Danny said, "Old Jim wants to see us; we are in trouble."

"Nah, maybe he wants to take us out for chow," I consoled him. "Let us go find out."

"All right, but you go first."

We went to his chambers; the door was open, and Old Jim saw us. "Come in, boys. I have something for you. Danny, how are you feeling?"

Danny was shaking and did not know what to say. "I'm fine, sir. And you?"

"I am glad to hear that. I'm feeling well, thank you. Now, I have half your pay here. I thought you might need it in New York."

Now I was shaking. Old Jim was giving us money. I didn't know what to say. "Thank you, sir."

"Well, you boys take care of yourselves. Be careful out there. This isn't Ireland! Good-bye, now."

Danny and I left, not sure what had happened. Old Jim had never spoken so many words to us. He must have known we would not be back. Both Danny and I knew that the crew never got paid until they returned to the ship's home port of Belfast. We left and found ourselves alone in the port of New York.

~ Getting Our Drums ~

One of the first things Danny did was find a newspaper and hand it to me. I looked at it; the date was May 24, 1846.

"Ian, what does it say? Is there anything about California? Ian, what is it? Tell me what it says!"

Danny was shaking me now. I looked at him and told him, "The United States is at war with Mexico. Mexican troops crossed a river called the Rio Grande, killed some US soldiers, and took the rest prisoner. President Polk has called for volunteers to meet the Mexican threat."

I saw that look in Danny's eyes. He was thinking about something, and I knew what it was. Then he said to me, "Why don't we volunteer?"

"What, are you mad? We're not even old enough!"

"Sure we are," he said. "I see boys younger than us in the British army. The president needs us."

There would be no talking him out of it. Once Danny had his mind set on something, that was it. Besides, the idea of war appealed to me. Putting on a uniform and becoming a hero was every boy's dream.

"Danny, let's go see if we can get some new boots and some food," I told him.

"We'll get the best marching boots in New York," Danny said. "Right, Ian?"

"We sure will; we'll be the best dressed, too."

We found some good boots. At an inn, we got some food, the best I had tasted since leaving Ireland. Old Jim had given us more than half our pay; we still had some left over. The lady who ran the inn was very nice. She did, however, insist that we take baths and would not take no for an answer. Danny and I both made it through the ordeal, and we spent the night at the inn.

It was not hard to find a recruiter. A line of men had already formed, so we just joined the line. Finally, it was our turn.

"What do you two want?" the recruiter asked us, and I answered him smartly.

"We want to join up to fight, sir."

"You have to be eighteen to enlist," was his rejoinder, but I was not discouraged.

"We can play the drums, sir."

"So you want to be musicians? There is no age limit on them. But you two have to be the youngest I've seen. You can have the job if you want it."

"Yes, sir, we will take it," I said with pride.

"Okay, give me your names."

"I am Ian Walsh, and this here is me friend Danny Higgins."

"You are now signed up," said the recruiter. "Report to the sergeant standing right behind me." So off we went to the sergeant, who was very tall.

"Sir," I said, "we're here to report for duty."

"Well now, what do we have here?" he mused in response. "You two are kind of short to be soldiers, aren't you?"

"No, we're not; I've whipped plenty—" Danny started to blurt out, but before he could finish, the sergeant broke in.

"Take it easy, lad, I'm just joshing you. You'll make a fine soldier. I am Sergeant Pat O'Reilly of the First New York."

"Danny Higgins, sir," replied Danny.

I yelled my name out next. "Ian Walsh!"

"You boys are from Ireland, I take it."

"Yes, we are, sir. Belfast."

"Well, I'm from Dublin myself. You will find most of the First New York came from Ireland, except our lieutenant; he's just out of West Point. Now, what I want you two to do is get in line over there for your uniforms. Later today, we head upstate to a training camp."

The rest of the day was nothing but hanging around in lines. Our uniforms were issued to us by the state of New York, and women had volunteered to fit us. The uniforms consisted of white pants with a red line down the sides, a blue jacket with red cuffs, a white shoulder belt, and a tall, blue hat with a black visor.

Next, we went over to an area to receive our drums. The drum hooked onto my shoulder belt, and the drumsticks could be tied to the drum when not in my hands.

A proud feeling came over me. I looked over at Danny, who had already started to play his drum. He was good, too. It seemed that things could not have been better. Later that day, I found myself at a camp in upstate New York.

The following morning, I woke up and joined the line for inspection. Lieutenant Michael Smith was our commanding officer and would be conducting the inspection. He was young but did not let that stop him. He took full charge of the troops.

Danny and I stood behind the regiment. The lieutenant approached us with Sergeant O'Reilly and spoke to Danny. "Hello, son. I heard you playing the drum; it was very good. What is your name?"

"Danny Higgins, sir."

"Are you Irish?" he asked.

"Yes, sir. I came over on a boat just the other day," Danny said proudly.

He turned to me next. "You are?"

"Ian Walsh, sir."

"You're Irish, too?"

"Yes, sir," I replied. "I came over on the same boat as Danny."

The lieutenant looked at Sergeant O'Reilly. "Is this a conspiracy, Sergeant? Not even the drummer boys are American."

"No, sir. They are good lads ... and besides, no one else volunteered for the job. Danny here already knows how to play the drums."

"Yes, I was listening to him play before; he is good, and I believe Ian will be, too, with some practice."

Sergeant O'Reilly looked pleased. "Aye, sir, I'll see to it."

"Good. Dismiss the men for chow and then start your drills; we have maybe two, three weeks at the most before we depart for New Orleans."

Camp was horrible; I could not wait to get out of there and get to New Orleans. From there, I learned, we could invade Mexico and put an end to the war. My drumming got better, thanks to Danny. We learned how to march in formation, too.

After days of marching around the training camp, the order finally came for us to move out. Danny brought the news to me. "Ian, I heard the lieutenant tell the sergeant that we would be heading out tomorrow for Pennsylvania to join up with some volunteers from there and then it's off to New Orleans. A General Winfield Scott has called for us."

I said to him, "This is it; we will be in Mexico after that ... and who knows, Danny? Maybe we will find the lost cities of gold."

This thrilled Danny. He said, "Then we would have it made— all the gold we could want, and nobody could tell me what to do."

I put a question to him: "Danny, what is the first thing you would do if you found all that gold?"

"I would buy the biggest tombstone for my mother's grave, and everyone would know a queen rested in that spot," was his reply.

"You didn't really know your mother, did you, Danny?"

"No, the only thing I do remember is how she would sing to me before I went to sleep and would stay with me 'til I fell asleep."

"I don't know what happened to my parents," I confided. "When our potato crop failed, I decided to go into Belfast to find a job to help out me dad. When I returned, there was nobody there, and I never did find a job."

"I am glad you are here with me, Ian," Danny said.

It was a long march to Pennsylvania, and I learned the importance of good boots. We met the Pennsylvanians at a small town called Gettysburg. After we pitched our tents and made camp, Danny and I went exploring in the town.

"What do you think of this town, Danny?"

"Not much here except a graveyard," he replied.

"Don't forget the farms; we might find some dairy cows for some fresh milk. But let us check out the graveyard first."

"I'll race you to the gates, Ian."

"Go!" I shouted.

We ran up to the street toward the gates leading into the cemetery and stopped. Danny did beat me but not by much. I looked up at the sign on top of the gate and turned to Danny. "You know what that sign says?"

"No. What, Ian?"

I read it to him: "'No discharging of firearms allowed on cemetery grounds.' I guess they don't want to wake up the dead."

Then the strangest thing happened to me; I thought my mind was going. I could hear screaming, but I saw nothing. I asked Danny if he heard anything.

"No," he said. "You aren't going mad on me?" he added in a sarcastic tone of voice.

"Maybe, Danny," I answered.

We went back to camp, only to sneak back out later and head for a nearby dairy farm that we had spotted.

"There they are, Ian—out in the field!" Danny screamed out.

"Quiet!" I told him. "We will creep up to the closest one and then leave."

I quietly walked up to one that was awake and started to pet her. After I won her confidence, I took my canteen and began to milk her. I looked up for Danny and did not see him at first, but I soon spotted him in the field.

"Danny," I called in a low voice. "Don't!" But it was too late; he had already sent the sleeping cow tumbling down.

Everything went out of control. The cow woke up and charged right at Danny, who started running toward me. A voice started yelling from the farmhouse, "Who's out there?" Then a shot rang out from the house. Both of us ran as fast as we could for the fence, dove over it, scrambled back to our feet, and headed for camp.

The next morning, we woke up for inspection. When that was completed, we sat down to eat. I still had the milk in my canteen and poured some into a pan and boiled it over the fire. I gave some to Danny in his tin cup and put the rest in mine.

While we were eating, Lieutenant Smith and Sergeant O'Reilly came over to us.

The lieutenant said to me, "It's a fine day, soldier."

"Yes, sir, it is," I replied. Something was not right, and a lump started to form in my throat.

"Did you sleep well last night?" he asked.

I thought I was going to lose my voice but managed to get out, "Yes, sir."

"Good, because I know that with the farms around here, it can be noisy and hard to sleep. But I made sure we were far enough away so we wouldn't be disturbed by cows or any other farm animals."

I was speechless as he just looked at me.

"What is that you are drinking, milk?" He picked up my cup and tasted it. "Fresh milk, I would say—right from the cow. I haven't tasted that in a long time. Sergeant, why don't you try some?"

"Thank you, sir. I will." The sergeant picked up Danny's cup and began to drink. "This sure is good, Lieutenant, sir. I think you are right—can't be more than a couple of hours out of the cow. Yes, sir, I grew up on a cow farm in Ireland. Funny thing about cows, sir: they sleep standing up, but if you give them a push, they roll right over."

"I didn't know that, Sergeant."

"Yes, sir, but when they get up, you better run for it. They will charge right at you, those mean-tempered cows."

"Well, Sergeant, I guess you'd be throwing up a storm if someone knocked you out of your bed."

"I sure would," said the sergeant.

Danny and I just sat with our mouths open, listening to them talk. The lieutenant and sergeant put the cups down. I looked in the cups, and both were empty. I looked up at the lieutenant, who winked at me and said, "Thank you, son. I enjoyed it."

Danny looked at me and said, "How do they do it?"

"What do you mean, Danny?"

"Grown-ups. How do they know everything?"

"I don't know, but me milk is all gone, and I never got to taste it."

"Mine's all gone, too," said Danny. "The sergeant didn't leave a drop."

I found out later that the farmer had complained to the lieutenant about someone disturbing his cows, but that was after our regiment with the Pennsylvanians headed for New Orleans.

~ The War ~

The road to New Orleans was long and tough on the feet. We marched eight to ten hours a day. The sun was hot and the roads dry, causing dirt to be kicked up and get all over us. It was a relief when we made it to the Mississippi River and took barges down to the Gulf of Mexico.

Christmas had been spent on the road, but we arrived in New Orleans in time to bring in the new year of 1847. Soldiers milled about everywhere, and more came in with the passing of each day. This city had one big party after another. The president had requested that the troops be entertained, so dancing girls were brought into the camps to put on shows, and that is what they did.

One night, I decided to slip out of camp and see for myself what really went on at night in New Orleans. I'd heard many stories about the city and wanted to see if they were true. I came to a street called Bourbon Street. I could hear music, singing, and laughter. Heading in the direction of the noise, I passed pub after pub. Standing on a crate that was outside of one pub, I peeked in to see what was going on inside. I looked through the window, I saw a man pick up a chair and throw it at a soldier, who ducked. The chair flew toward the window I was looking through, and I jumped down off the crate at a run. Behind me came a big crash.

Not looking where I was going, I ran into a mass of green, almost losing my balance. When I looked up, I saw a lady in the brightest green dress with the darkest blue lace, laughing at me.

"What's your hurry, soldier boy?"

"Nuh … nuh … nothing, ma'am," I just barely managed to get out.

"Say, aren't you a little young to be a soldier?" she asked.

"I'm a musician, ma'am."

"Oh, well, do you have any money on you?"

She was still smiling at me. I didn't really know what she was getting at, but I told her, "I have two dollars, ma'am."

"Well, now. For two dollars, I could give you a music lesson you will never forget."

I had two options to choose from: receive a music lesson or run and not stop until I got to camp. But before I could make a decision, a soldier came over. "Sweetie, you want a real man, not a squirt of a kid," he said and pushed me out of the way as the two of them walked off. She kept looking back at me, giggling the whole time. I never forgot that green dress and would be glad later that I did wait for my music lesson. I sneaked back into camp and fell asleep.

The time came when we were to move into Mexico. It was February. Ships came and took us to an island off the coast of

Mexico. The city of Vera Cruz was our target. General Scott arrived on the island soon after us and prepared for the invasion.

When enough boats had arrived, we landed about three miles south of the city and surrounded it. Our artillery bombed the city all day, and the Navy did the same from the sea. The noise of gunfire and smell of gunpowder filled the air. It was hard to get used to, but after a while, I became numb to it. After six days, the city surrendered, and we began the move toward Mexico City. Until then, Danny and I had not seen any fighting, just fireworks.

About fifty miles inland, in a village called Cerro Gordo, the Mexicans tried to turn us back. Our regiment arrived early in the morning under the command of General Worth. Danny and I were told by Sergeant O'Reilly to report to Major Paul Preston. He was the regiment's doctor. We helped him set up for the wounded, but the battle went well for us, and our regiment did not see any action. By the end of the day, the village was ours. Over three thousand Mexicans had surrendered to us.

The next place we stopped was Jalapa. I was tired and told Danny I was going to get some water and write in my diary before I turned in. I had walked out to the well, gotten some water, and sat down when I noticed a bright light on top of a hill. I made my way to the hill and started the climb up. The light got brighter and brighter. I found myself drawn to it and climbed faster to reach it. Finally, I reached the top and saw a city that was made of gold and sparkled in the light radiating from the stars.

I walked down the middle of the city, looking at the gold, and came to what looked like a door leading in to what seemed to be a castle. I tried the door, but it would not open. A spear leaned against the outside of the castle. I picked it up and wedged it into a crack in the door. I pushed with all my strength, and the door flew open. I went flying inside only to land on my butt. All around me were treasures that I had thought only existed in my dreams. Getting up, I moved farther into the castle. I discovered rooms filled with the most beautiful pottery, all painted in the brightest colors and lined in gold.

In one room was a table full of fruit. I was starving and ran up to the table, picking up the largest peach I could find. I took a bite, and then another. Suddenly, I noticed that the table the peach had been on had shrunk, but it was not the table; it was me. I was standing on air. With each bite I took, I went higher. I put my hands up to stop myself from crashing into the ceiling—I was so high—but there was nothing there. I passed right through what I had thought was the ceiling.

I found myself standing on a solid floor, looking at a pile of gold coins. There must have been thousands. *If only Danny were here to see this,* I thought. I lay back on the pile and just imagined what I was going to do with all the gold. Staring up at the ceiling above me, I took in its grandeur. Then I noticed the ceiling had begun to move, and my skin started to feel hot. I sat up in a hurry and found myself in a pile of scorpions; they were dropping from the ceiling onto me. My skin was burning, and I had no way out.

"Aghhhh … !"

"Ian! Ian! Wake up, son. It's okay." It was Major Preston. "Son, it's okay. You're burning up with fever."

"A fever!" It felt as if I were on fire. "The scorpions are all over me. Can't you see them?"

"No, you had a bad dream; that is all," he said. "A fever will do that. You'll be okay. More than half the regiment has it."

"What is it, Major Preston?"

"It's what we call dysentery. You'll feel bad for a while. You might even prefer the scorpions to this."

"I think I better dig myself a hole, because I'm—" was all I managed to blurt out.

"Say no more! Danny and some of the others have all ready dug some holes. Let me point you in the right direction."

I found a hole at the same time my stomach let go of everything. It felt as if someone were wringing every last drop of water out of my body. For the next two days, all I could do was lie down, except for the occasional run to my hole in the ground.

Danny finally came by to see me. "You look a lot better, Ian; I brought something to drink. The major said it would be all right. He found you asleep by the well."

"I'm really thirsty. What is it?"

"Tea. I got it in New Orleans. It's what I have been drinking. That is why I never got sick."

"Tea … how is that, Danny?"

"Well, the British army drinks it," he answered, "and I never heard of them getting sick."

I didn't quite follow his reasoning, but I was so thirsty I would have tried anything. "All right, I'll try some."

He poured some out of his canteen into my cup. I picked it up and took a sip. It was the worst tea I ever tasted. "Danny, how did you make this tea?"

"Well, I did not have any sugar or cream, so it is a bit strong."

"Thank you," I said, grateful despite the bitterness of the beverage.

After about six days, I was walking around and had started to eat again. I met Danny at the campfire, where he was getting ready to make some more tea. He took a small pot of water and stuck it in the fire until the water boiled. After that, he pulled the pot out and added the tea. After allowing the tea to steep for a few minutes, he poured it into his canteen.

"Ian, you want some for your canteen?"

As bad as the tea tasted, Danny was not sick, and no way did I want to get sick again. So I took some.

By the time two weeks had passed, my body felt almost back to normal. I did a lot of walking around and met a group of soldiers from South Carolina. Their captain was a Mr. Robert Shaw. He was a pleasant man and invited me to stay for chow one evening. That was the evening I was introduced to goober peas. They were tan in color, fat at the ends, and skinny in the middle. Their texture was rough, and when I took a bite, the taste was so bad I spit it out. A South Carolina soldier started laughing at me.

"That's not how you eat them things, boy. First, you got to crack the shell open and find the two goobers."

So I did, and covered in what looked like brown paper were two white goobers. They were hard and chewy, and they could have used some salt.

Later on I met a Captain Robert E. Lee, who was telling a story about the trail he had found back at Cerro Gordo. I stopped to listen.

"I had been separated from the other two officers who were with me. Heading back toward the American line, I heard horses coming in the distance. The only thing I could do was to hide under this rock that had been eroded away on one side. So I squeezed myself under it and waited for the horses to pass. But they didn't pass; they stopped. Getting off their horses, the Mexicans sat down right on top of the rock I was hiding under. The next thing I knew, they were eating lunch on top of the rock. I just stayed silent and hoped they would leave."

I had to ask him, "Did they leave?"

"No. And to make matters worse, right in front of my face, not more than an inch away, pops up a scorpion out of the sand. He was staring me straight in the face."

"What did you do?" I asked.

"Stared right back at him to let him know I was in charge. We both stayed frozen like that for almost an hour. The Mexicans finally left, and so did I. Can you believe that?"

"Yes," I replied, and told him all about my run-in with the scorpions. The rest of the men started to laugh and make jokes about me, but Captain Lee put his hand on my shoulder.

"Son," he said, "what's your name?"

"Ian Walsh, sir. I am from the First New York—a musician, sir."

"I bet a good one, too. You pay these men no mind. I believe you. Next time you meet a scorpion, just stare him in the eyes, and don't let him see your fear."

With so many men sick, General Scott had decided to halt the advance and stay in Jalapa, but when May came, it was time to move on. We entered the city of Puebla, and I saw no signs of a fight or the Mexican army. Puebla was no better than Jalapa. Men were falling sick just as fast, and Major Preston said he thought it was the water. It didn't matter much to me. I was still drinking tea, and neither Danny nor I got sick.

The red sandstone was a grand sight to see, but it was tough on clothing. By then, most of our uniforms had a reddish color to them, with the white pants being the worst.

It was not until the end of August that we moved again. Early in the morning, our regiment was awakened and ordered to move out. Dawn had just broken when we reached our destination.

Lieutenant Smith ordered us in battle line formation facing a ridge, where I could see a large formation of Mexican troops. Lieutenant Smith gave the order: "Fix bayonets!" Then he raised his sword and gave a nod to Danny, which was the signal to start the drum roll. I would follow Danny's lead. I realized then that I was about to experience my first battle. Until then, all I had done was march.

Lieutenant Smith turned to me. "Play, Ian, so they will be able to hear you in Mexico City." So I did. Then the artillery started to fire; it lasted for ten minutes and then stopped. From the top of the ridge, arose American troops that maneuvered themselves behind the Mexican lines, they charged. Within a few minutes, it was all over, and the Mexicans were running with our cavalry right behind them.

I looked up at Lieutenant Smith. He gave me a wink and said, "Not today."

Danny and I took a tea break later that evening. "Ian, were you scared today?" he asked me.

"Aye. I thought we were really going to charge up that ridge."

"It was a grand show, was it not?" Danny asked.

"It was," I said, "and I bet you that Captain Lee had something to do with it."

"Maybe. How about telling me a story?"

I nodded to him. "I will tell you a story I heard in Jalapa. It's about a Mexican boy living outside of Mexico City on a huge plantation. His father was one of the richest people in Mexico. He went to the best school in the city. All his classmates looked up to him. On his plantation, he had started his own zoo. He captured some birds, lizards, and a coyote—his most recent addition."

"Ian, what's a coyote?" Danny interrupted.

"It is something like a dog, but it's wild," I said. "Everyone had told him that he would not be able to tame the coyote. Now, the coyote was still very young when he found it. He was determined to show everyone that they were wrong. His father tried to tell him that it was a wild, murderous animal and should be killed before it got too big. He would not listen.

"One night he overheard his father talking to his mother, saying he would have to take the coyote out and shoot it before it became too dangerous. The boy knew that there was only one thing he could do. He had to take the coyote and hide in the mountains. The boy did that, and to this day, people have seen the boy and his coyote in the mountains around Mexico City."

"You made that up!"

"No, it's the truth; you might even see them, Danny."

"Maybe," Danny doubtfully conceded. "Did you see this notice?" he asked, holding out a leaflet. "There are a lot of them lying around."

"No, I haven't. Let me see what it says."

He handed the leaflet over. "Here. I could not read it, but I know it has a Hail Mary in Latin at the bottom."

"It reads: 'To all Catholics, do not fight against your fellow Catholics. Join us, and the Mexican government will reward you with land and money. We are all one family.' Then it has a Hail Mary and is signed by Santa Anna himself."

"Everybody wants us to fight for them, Ian. The British say we are British and send us all over the world to fight for them. The nationalists want us to fight for Ireland against the British. President Polk asks us to fight for the United States. And now Mexico wants us to join them. We're pretty popular."

"The United States is our country now, Danny. We left the nationalists and the British behind, and for the first time, we belong. We are free for the first time. Besides, the Mexicans can't win. They don't fight together. I heard Lieutenant Smith say you can't win a war with too many generals, each of whom is trying to win the war on his own."

Danny seemed unconvinced. "I don't know, Ian. What do you say we go over to the South Carolina camp and get some goober peas?"

"Don't you ever get sick of them?" I asked him. "They do something to my stomach."

"Nah, they're great. Let's go."

So I went to get some goober peas.

The next day, I woke up to find that a battle had started at a church the Mexicans had turned into a fort. By the time our regiment arrived, the fighting had stopped. But I saw the results. We had taken the worst beating of the war so far. I heard that close to a thousand men had been lost, but the Mexicans were on the retreat again, and we were following right behind them.

Our advancement stopped just outside of Mexico City. It was September, and on the seventh, the fighting resumed. Once again, the First New York did not see any fighting. We were outside the Mexican Military College when our artillery started a bombardment. On the following day, the infantry would make its assault.

Early in the morning, the First New York positioned themselves to attack. I knew that this time, we would be in the fight. Lieutenant Smith raised his sword, looked at Danny and me, and gave the order to advance. To our drums, the New Yorkers moved into battle. The path to the castle was a steep climb, but we moved on. The closer we got, the heavier the gunfire became. As we neared the castle, I saw men lying lifeless on the ground.

They did not move and would not ever move again. I knew some of them; others I did not. Then I was standing outside the castle, looking up at the walls.

I heard Sergeant O'Reilly. "Bring the bloody ladder up here."

"Sir, we left them down there," answered a soldier, who then pointed down the hill we had just climbed.

"What? I'm working with a bunch of fools! We'll have to find another way in."

"Sergeant, over here I found an open gate," shouted a soldier. "We can get in through it."

We entered the castle to find everyone was running everywhere inside. Americans were pouring over the wall. Most of the Mexicans could not have been much older than I was. In all the confusion, I was hit from behind and fell to the ground. I lay on my back, and standing over me was a boy dressed in a green, red, and white uniform. He had a saber raised over his head, and it started a downward dive straight for me. My drum was my only weapon, and I swung it around on top of my chest. The saber hit it and deflected off, hitting the dirt and getting stuck in the ground. Red, swollen, watery eyes were looking at me. He let go of the saber and ran off.

An American soldier came over and lowered his hand down to me. I grabbed it and was pulled to my feet. "You all right?" he asked. I nodded, and he took off. The confusion seemed to go on and on all day long, but it finally came to an end. The Mexicans surrendered, and the American flag flew over the castle. There was nothing else between us and Mexico City, the war was over.

It was at this time that I noticed Danny sitting on his drum with his right leg stretched out. I went over to see what had happened to him.

"Danny, what's the matter with you?"

"I can't walk. My foot … there's something wrong with it."

I bent over to look at it. Just above his right ankle was a nice, round hole in his boot. Blood was oozing out it.

"Danny, I think you have been shot. You have to get to Major Preston." I helped him to his feet, letting him lean on me so that no pressure was put on his foot.

Sergeant O'Reilly saw us and came running over. "What is wrong, lad?" He glanced down at Danny's foot and picked him up in his big arms. "Don't worry, lad. I'll take you to Major Preston; he'll fix you up."

I followed behind them. Major Preston had already set up a hospital inside the castle. Sergeant O'Reilly put Danny down on a table, and Major Preston came over. "What did you do to yourself, Danny?" he asked.

"I don't know, sir; it just happened like that."

At that point, Major Preston cut off Danny's boot with a knife. The boot was covered with blood.

"Where did it happen?" he asked Danny.

"I think when we were charging up the hill."

"And you still climbed up the hill?" asked Major Preston, seemingly impressed.

"Yes, sir. I had to keep playing the drum. Right, Sergeant O'Reilly?"

"Aye, lad," the sergeant said. "You just listen to the major, now."

"I don't know how you were still able to walk on this foot," the major commented. "It is in bad shape; you had a bullet go right through. Ian, I want you to stay here with Danny. I will be right back."

"So maybe you will get a medal, Danny," I told him.

"You think so?"

"Aye, I do."

"I'm scared, though. You won't leave me?"

"I won't. I'll stay right here and make sure you're all right."

"Thanks, Ian. I am feeling sleepy and cold."

"Well, don't go to sleep on me."

Major Preston returned with two orderlies and his tools. I knew what it meant, and I knew Danny did, too. Major Preston finally looked at me and said, "Ian, I'm sorry, but his foot has to come off. I'm sorry. I wish there were another way."

Danny looked at me and said, "Don't worry. It will be all right."

One of the orderlies took off his leather belt and told Danny to bite down on it as he put it into his mouth. Major Preston had told me to hold Danny's right hand.

"Danny, everything is going to be fine. I will make sure of it," I told him.

It took Major Preston only a few minutes to do what he had to do. Danny held on to my hand so tightly that my fingers turned white and became numb. I used all of my weight to keep his arm down.

When it was over, Danny had a smile on his face.

"Don't let go of me hand," he said. "I feel so cold."

His hand felt cold, and he was still holding onto mine so tightly that there was no way I could let go. "I'm not going anywhere, Danny," I said.

"It wasn't too bad, Ian. I'm not afraid anymore. I can hear my mother singing to me. It is just as I remember. She would sing away all of my fears, so I could sleep. I'm not afraid to go to sleep now, Ian. Mommy is here … Mommy … Mom!"

"No, no, no, Danny!" I shouted, but his grip on my hand slackened and released.

I was grabbed from behind in a bear hug; it was Major Preston. "Son, he's gone. I did everything I could. It was just too much for his tiny body to handle, and he should never have had to. I'm sorry, Ian. There was just nothing more that I could do."

I stood there and watched as they took Danny away. Then I went and got my drum. That afternoon we marched in Mexico City. I kept looking on my left, expecting to see Danny, but he was not there. I was the lone musician of the First New York.

~ A New Lifestyle ~

There was a big celebration in Mexico City that night. I found a quiet place to sit and be alone. I tried to go to sleep, but every time I did, I found myself in a dark room with nothing in it. Then I would hear screams and laughing. I would find a door to escape, but it only opened into another dark, empty room. The screams and laughter would become so loud that I would wake up in a sweat, and my ears would be ringing. It was only a dream, but it seemed so real. This dream continued to haunt me every night.

Lieutenant Smith found me one day and wanted to know how I was faring. "Ian, I heard what happened. I am sorry. How are you making out?"

"All right, sir."

"What have you been doing with yourself?"

"I have no plans, sir."

"Now that the war is over, what are your plans?"

"I don't know. Maybe go to California." But there was no reason for me to go there anymore.

"I met a friend of yours today," said the lieutenant. "Captain Robert Shaw. He asked me why you haven't been by for some goober peas. He wants you to stop by and see him."

"All right, sir. I will."

I went to see Captain Shaw. He was inside one of the houses and, yes, he was eating goober peas.

"Who is it?" I heard a voice ask from behind a desk.

"Ian, sir, Lieutenant Smith said you wanted to see me."

"Yes, come in, Ian." I entered the room.

"Do you have plans now?" he asked.

"I don't know what I want to do, sir. I had thought of going to California."

"Would you like to come with me to Charleston, South Carolina? I have a shipping company, and I'm always looking for help at the docks."

"I don't know what to say, sir. I've never been so confused."

"Why don't you take some time to think about it? I'll be here for three more days."

I needed help. Until that point in my life, I had always known what to do.

I went to see Lieutenant Smith. Somehow I knew that he would know what I should do. I found him reading the newspaper under a tree, and I walked over and sat down next to him. He looked down at me and then went back to reading the paper.

"Ian," he said, "President Polk is sending someone to negotiate the terms of the peace treaty."

"It's all over, isn't it, sir?"

"Yes, it is, Ian. Now you have to move into another part of your life."

"I wish it didn't have to end."

"But it has ended. Trying to keep it alive will not change what happened."

I knew he was right. "How's Charleston, South Carolina?" I blurted out.

"I hear the weather is good, and they have some of the best fishing in the United States."

"I think I'll go there next. Captain Shaw invited me."

"He is a good man, Ian. You must have made a good impression on him."

"Thank you, sir."

I told Captain Shaw I would go and try it out. I knew I could always leave.

The day before I was going to Charleston, Lieutenant Smith asked me if I wanted to go to the stores in the city to buy some new clothes. The only clothing I had was the uniform given to me, so I went. By then Mexico City was filled with Americans trying to make money off the soldiers. Lieutenant Smith bought me a new suit with a bow tie and a pair of shoes. Then we went to what looked like an inn and met a Senora Diaz. She only spoke Spanish, so Lieutenant Smith did all the talking. I had no idea what they were saying. I just stood there with my box, which had my new clothes in it. The next thing I knew, I was being led into a room with a tub right in the middle. Before I could say anything, Lieutenant Smith left, saying, "I'll wait for you outside."

I soon found myself in a tub full of hot water and soap, which smelled very sweet.

I said, "No!" which I was sure was the same in Spanish, but Senora Diaz did not seem to understand. The worst part was when the brush came. It had to have been made from the needles of a cactus. Finally, it was over. I put on my new clothes and went out to see Lieutenant Smith.

"Ian, is that you? I almost didn't recognize you."

"Yes, sir, it is. Do you think Captain Shaw will recognize me?" For the first time in my life, I felt like somebody, and I was proud of my new suit.

"He may or may not, but I will go with you, just in case."

The next morning, I got up early and went with Lieutenant Smith to meet Captain Shaw. He had a wagon to take us to Vera Cruz, where one of his ships was waiting to take us to Charleston.

"Well, I'll be danged. Is this Ian Walsh, Lieutenant?"

"Sure is, Captain."

"Gosh, with that outfit, black hair, and blue eyes, he'll have all the girls in Charleston after him."

It was grand to see the high seas again. The ship we were on was called the *King David.* It was bigger than the *Courageous* and even had rooms. I had one all to myself. There was no work for me to do. I just sat back and enjoyed the trip. The crew referred to me as Master Walsh.

In a few days, we were heading into Charleston Harbor. Guarding it was a fort, and the captain of the ship told me it was Fort Sumter. This was going to be one exciting adventure! At the docks, a carriage was waiting to take Captain Shaw and me to the Shaws' residence.

The carriage pulled up and stopped at a huge, red brick house. Steps led up to the front door. Looking behind me, I could see the harbor. I went up the steps with Captain Shaw; he opened the door, and we went in. Waiting inside for us were three people. Captain Shaw introduced them.

"Ian, this is my wife, Joan; my daughter, Lisa; and this is Maggie, our housekeeper."

Mrs. Shaw spoke next. "Robert, I didn't know you were bringing home a guest."

"Yes, this is the surprise I wrote to you about. I told him he could live with us for as long as he wishes."

"Oh, this is a surprise!" I could tell that Mrs. Shaw had not been expecting another addition to the family so soon. "Well, welcome, Ian. I'll have Maggie get a room ready."

"A room for me, ma'am?" I was shocked by their hospitality.

"Yes, with your own bed."

"That's not necessary, ma'am."

Mrs. Shaw smiled kindly. "Of course it is. You're part of the family now."

A room with a bed was more than I could ever imagine. I had never slept in a bed before. The bunk on the ship over from Ireland had been luxurious, and now a bed. I spotted a staircase leading to another floor. This house had *two* floors in it.

Captain Shaw saw me looking at the stairs. "Well, do you want to explore the house, Ian?"

"Yes, I do, sir."

"Well, go ahead."

I started with the stairs, running as fast as I could to get to the top. As I approached the top, a wooden cane appeared in front of me, tripping me up and landing me flat on my stomach. I turned my head, looking up. There was a man standing there in a gray suit with a tall, gray hat. His hair was slightly gray, and he had a gray beard.

He walked by me down the stairs, singing, "We don't run in the house anymore; we don't run in the house anymore." That was how I met Mr. Robert Shaw Senior, whom I would later call Grandpa Shaw.

Getting to my feet and looking at the bottom of the stairs, I saw Lisa Shaw giggling, and she said to me, "You're funny and cute."

The last thing I needed, as a thirteen-year-old boy, was an eleven-year-old girl thinking I was cute. "Funny" I could take, but "cute"? She had the prettiest blonde hair, blue eyes, and freckles. I was going to be in trouble.

Later that evening, I sat down for dinner with the Shaw family. Captain Shaw started dinner with a prayer. "We give you thanks, Lord, for the food we are about to eat and for bringing Ian into our family. Amen."

The dinner consisted of pork, biscuits, rice, and cabbage, which made me feel right at home. Everything was served on fine china, and even the individual dinner plates were made of it. Maggie had filled my plate, and I was ready to eat. Not knowing any other way to eat but with my hands, I picked up my food.

But then quietness fell over the table. Everyone had their eyes fixed on me.

It could be only one thing, so I said the only thing I could: "We don't eat with our hands in the house anymore."

Trying his best to keep a straight face, Captain Shaw answered, "Yes, that is correct. We use the silver that is next to our plates instead."

I knew what those things were for. Maggie came over and showed me how to use them.

After dinner it was time to retire to my room. I climbed into my bed, and it was more than decadent, but I still could get no sleep. That dream of the empty rooms and laughter haunted me even in Charleston. Even with all these comforts, I could not escape it.

The following day was Sunday. It was time to go to church, so I put on my best suit and arrived with the Shaw family at a church that I suddenly realized was not the right church. It was not a *Catholic* church!

Everyone was entering when I said to Grandpa Shaw, "I'll wait outside, if you don't mind, sir." I knew that something awful would happen to me if I went in.

"Nonsense. Come in and sit down with us."

I dug my heels into the ground. Grandpa Shaw just put his hand on my back, and I went through the door. My eyes were shut tight, waiting for the worst to happen, but nothing did. I opened them.

It was a plain church, and everything was white. No statues or stained glass windows were to be found. The service started with singing. Then a man got up and went to the pulpit. He opened the Bible and read from it. No Latin was spoken.

The man closed the Bible and started to preach: "The devil is at work in Charleston. Yes, he takes many forms, but let us not be fooled. He will disguise his evil deeds, so they appear to be good. No, my people! Let us not be fooled. The Bible is our guide; Jesus's life is the example we must follow. The Almighty God is all good and powerful! Obliterate sin from your lives, and turn to God for your Salvation now!"

"Alleluia!" I shouted.

All eyes in the church focused on me. Grandpa Shaw pulled me back into my seat and whispered into my ear, "Not now. I will tell you when."

The service ended. Outside I was introduced to many people. The Reverend came over to say hello. Captain Shaw introduced him to me.

"Ian, I'd like you to meet Reverend Johnstone."

"Hello, sir."

"Hello, Ian. I see my sermon inspired you."

"Sorry, sir. I did not mean to interrupt you."

"That is all right. It shows you were listening. Maybe even woke a few people up."

Once we had arrived back at home, it was time for the Sunday meal. There seemed to be no end to the food. As I lay in bed that night, I thought about how welcome I had been in that church. Why could it not have been that way in Ireland?

The Shaws were more than nice to me. I felt like part of the family, though I kept to myself most of the time. That nightmare still haunted me. I kept busy, hoping it would go away.

But my first problem was avoiding Lisa, who always seemed to be wherever I was. I refrained from running in the house and soon discovered that, although there was only one way up the stairs, there were two ways down. You could walk or take the banister, the second of which was much faster and came in handy when you were being chased.

The question that I was hoping would never come finally did: what about school? I tried to avoid it as long as possible, but Grandpa Shaw was quite convincing. He had already made arrangements to send me not just to school, but to a military academy.

It was Monday morning, and I was already awake when Grandpa Shaw came into my room to get me for school. He had already purchased my cadet uniform. It was plain and all one color, a bluish gray. The school was located in the center of the city. We arrived early in the morning. It was already the beginning of December, and 1848 was not far away. I had missed half the school year, but it did not matter to Grandpa Shaw. He wanted me in this school, and he got his way, as usual.

The commandant of the school was a Mr. Gary Dodd. He took me to the room where I would be staying. It had two beds, two desks, and two chairs, and I would be sharing it with a roommate. Mine would be Adam Cooper. He was eleven years old and had dark brown hair and brown eyes. Mr. Dodd told him to take me with him to all his classes and show me around later.

Adam already knew who I was, along with the rest of the school. Mr. Dodd had told them that a new student would be starting that day. No one talked to me but Adam. I did not have much to say to anyone anyway, so it was just as well. Adam had told me he would help me catch up on the work that I had missed.

The beginning of the week continued along the same lines. I kept to myself, and nobody bothered me. Wednesday night came. I returned to my room after doing some reading at the library to find Adam shining a pair of boots. From the size of them, it was obvious they were not his.

"Adam, whose boots are those?" I asked.

"They belong to Ned Hunter."

"Why are you polishing them for him?"

"Because if I don't, he will have me roasted—or worse."

I was confused. "Do you always do this for him?"

"Yes."

"How come I haven't been asked to polish his boots?"

He paused for a few seconds and then answered, "Well, all the cadets are afraid of you, so they try to avoid you."

"But why should they be afraid of me?"

"You were in the war with Mexico, and there is a rumor going around that you killed a bunch of Mexicans—one with your bare hands."

This was all news to me. After all, I had been only twelve then and had only been a musician. "Do you believe them, Adam?"

"No, you didn't kill anyone," he told me. "I hear you talk when you sleep, but most of the time, I see you sitting up in your bed, staring at the wall in the dark. A night monster has you."

"What is a night monster?"

"Each one is different," he said reverently. "My mother told me they get into your dreams and cause you to have terrible nightmares, so you can't sleep."

"How can I get rid of it?"

"I don't know. Each one is different, but all of them have one thing that can destroy them. All you have to do is find out what that is for *your* monster." He stood up and started for the door.

"Where are you going, Adam?"

"I am going to return Ned's boots to him."

I had an idea, so I said, "I will do that, Adam. I would like to meet him."

On the way to Ned's, I made a stop at the kitchen. I looked all around until I saw it: honey.

The next day came around, and I went to all my classes as usual. Evening came. Adam went to the library, and I stayed in the room to write. I left the door open and could see out to the door of the library. I figured on some visitors coming by, and they did. Ned Hunter and two other boys, Cory Hendricks and Paul Willis, went into the library, and I knew they were not there to read. I got up, went over to the library, and opened the door.

Ned greeted me first. "Leave, Paddy. This doesn't concern you."

I had not been called that for a long time—not since I had left Belfast, where fighting had been the one thing I knew how to do. I had had no choice but to fight on the streets of Belfast. The Protestant boys had laid into me many times. They liked to hear a Catholic boy say a Hail Mary and would wallop him until he did.

Ned, Cory, and Paul had never fought in their lives. They had always relied on others' fear of them. So I interrupted Ned and told him, "Yes, it does. I put the honey in your boots."

Adam looked at me in total surprise, along with Cory and Paul, who had not planned on me being their target. But Ned had no problem answering back. "Well, it looks like we roast Paddy tonight."

Now, roasting consisted of holding someone up against the hot bricks of a fireplace, but I was not about to be roasted. Ned stepped forward, taking a swing at me, and I ducked. He had swung so hard that he lost his balance, falling over a chair. Once up on his feet, he tried to frighten me.

"Now we will really teach you a lesson!"

There was that word that had gotten me into trouble before. I could never understand it, the universal *we*. Ned had never asked Cory or Paul their thoughts on this subject, but Ned, with that one word, had spoken for them. Before I knew it, the three of them were on top of me. Somehow I managed to free myself and was kneeling in front of them, with the three of them still tangled up on the ground. Cory was the first one to start to get up. Before he could get to his feet, I clenched my fist, still kneeling, and let go with everything I had. I hit him square on the chin, sending him flat on his back. I wound up on my stomach but quickly got to my feet. My next punch was for Ned himself, along with the following four punches as well.

Paul, living up to his reputation for being a coward, took off for the door just before Major Roberts came in, broke up the fight, and took us to see Mr. Dodd. Blood dripped down my chin from the cut on my lip. Mr. Dodd took one look at us and told us to clean up and report to him first thing in the morning.

Adam was still up when I returned to the room.

"Ian," he said, "you really lived up to your reputation!"

But I was forlorn. "I made a mess of things, I know."

"No, he had it coming to him. But why did you put honey in his boots?"

"I don't know. The boots were in my hands. I saw the honey, and it just happened."

Adam laughed and said, "Good night."

The next day, I reported to Mr. Dodd and found Cory already there. Ned was not. After classes we were to report to the square and stand at attention for two hours. We left for our classes.

I asked Cory where Ned was, and he told me that Ned had been expelled. It occurred to me that Cory had told Mr. Dodd everything about what Ned had been doing. He was rubbing his sore chin.

"Cory, I'm sorry," I said to him.

"Ian, it wasn't your fault, but did you have to hit me so hard?"

"I went crazy, I guess."

"You sure did."

Cory was to become my best friend. Neither one of us had said anything about Paul being there, so he was spared.

The week finally came to an end. Everyone was getting ready to go home for the weekend. I thought I might head west. My bags were packed. I was all ready, but waiting outside for me was Grandpa Shaw with a black puppy. He called to me. "Ian, son, hurry up. I have something to show you. What do you think of my new Lab? I'm going to need some help teaching him to be a duck dog."

"He's a grand puppy, sir. A wee thing, though."

"Don't you worry—he will get bigger. Why don't you hold him and think of a name for me?"

So I held him, and he started licking my face all over. It was turning into a great day for me.

"So, Ian, how was your first week at school? See any good brawls lately?"

"No, but I was in one," I said sheepishly.

"Yes, I heard. Mr. Dodd said you really gave it to Ned Hunter. Wish I could have been there. I can't stand that boy's father. He's in that evil slave business."

"You aren't mad, sir?"

"No, Ian. Let me tell you about the legend of Little Fox. He was the son of a chief. He did everything his father and mother told him to do. There was one thing, though, that he was afraid of: the forest.

"He had never had to go into the forest alone, but his thirteenth birthday came along. That meant that he was a man and, by custom, he must spend a week in the forest all by himself. He never told anyone about his fear. How could he? He was the son of a chief; no fear could be shown. His cowardice would break his father's heart and make him the laughingstock of the tribe.

"The day came for him to set out on his own. All he could take was his spear. Deeper and deeper he went into the forest. He made many new friends in the forest. One day he fell asleep under a big oak tree. Usually he kept alert, but sleep finally overtook him. A mighty roar woke him just in time to see a bear charging toward him. The only thing he could do was climb up the oak tree. The bear leaped up after him, only to get himself wedged between two branches. The branches were so strong that they held the bear there. They had the bear around the neck. The more the bear struggled to get free, the tighter the branches got around his neck. Before long the bear had suffocated itself.

"Little Fox returned to the tribe with the bear's skin wrapped around him. He was hailed as a hero, and his father was very proud of him. He had faced his fears and was no longer afraid of the forest. It could no longer have a hold on him. He was free."

"I wish it were that easy, sir."

"Don't worry. When the time comes, you will know what to do. You have to do it on your own. It's the only way."

That night I took the black Lab up to my room to sleep. It may have been a mistake, but I did not care.

At about six in the morning, I was being slobbered on. It was time for the puppy to go for a walk. I got dressed and was ready to take him outside when I saw my boots. They had been chewed to pieces and no longer resembled boots. They had made it through the Mexican War and never failed me, but they had fallen to the wrath of a teething puppy. Suddenly, it came to me: his name would be Boots!

After breakfast, Maggie called me to say that there was someone at the front door for me. I went to the door, not knowing who it was. Cory Hendricks was standing there in old clothes, with no shoes on, and two poles in his hand.

"Ian, I am going fishing if you want to come."

I had never been fishing before, but I did want to go. "Sure, Cory. Can I bring Boots?" The dog had followed me to the door.

"Why, sure you can." Cory led me through some woods until we came to a lake. The lake was a good size. He took me to a place on the bank and then said, "This is the best spot to fish, and nobody knows about it except me ... and now you. I usually come here when I want to be alone."

I learned all about catfish: how to catch them, clean them, and cook them. "So, Ian," Cory asked, "how do you like fishing?"

"It's all right."

"I shouldn't have followed Ned," he confided.

"Why did you, Cory?"

"Because I found it was easier to follow him than go against him. I'm not like you, Ian. Everything is always done for me. My father sees to that. You know he is the best lawyer in Charleston? He serves as a state legislator. I never made a choice on my own. You changed all that. It's like I was playing hide and seek, and you took away the bed I was hiding under. I will never be able to hide again."

I was surprised. "You are not mad at me for that?"

"No. I'm glad you did it. But there is one thing I would like to ask you, if you don't mind."

"No, I guess not."

"What happened in Mexico?"

Something about Cory and what he said did something to me. I just opened up and told him everything. For the first time, I relived the day Danny died. Without warning, something occurred that had never happened to me before. My eyes watered at first. Then it was like a rain came, and I could not stop it. A salty taste entered my mouth. Boots came over to lick the tears from my face. Cory sat there and just listened.

I finally was able to speak again, saying, "I guess I'm going soft, Cory."

"We all need to go soft at times. You know, Danny was right. Everything will be all right now."

I did not understand what Cory meant. Fishing did not turn out the way I thought it would, but I had a lot of fun. The three of us—Cory, Boots, and me—wound up getting all wet.

When I got back to the Shaws' house, I was a mess and had to take a bath. The lake's mud was packed all over me, and my clothes were soaked with lake water. Boots was on his way to becoming a duck dog. He was a natural in the water, and I told Grandpa Shaw.

It had been a long day for me. I was tired, something I always seemed to feel lately. I went to sleep and found myself in that dark room again, with the screams and laughter. Finding the door to run out, I expected to enter another dark room for more of the same. This time, however, when I opened the door, it was not another dark, empty room. I found myself on a ship, and I was the captain. I could go anywhere. I could look for buried treasures on uncharted islands; do battle with the most vicious sea monsters and come out on top; or rescue princesses from treacherous pirates. Yes, I was at the helm, in control of my dreams and my destiny once again. That was what Cory had meant when he said everything would be all right. The night monsters would never bother me again. I had faced my worst fear; by saying good-bye to Danny, I had broken its hold on me. There would be other battles, but I would now be able to fight them.

Sunday night I returned to the school and went to my room. Adam was already there when I arrived.

"You won, Ian."

Adam knew, I guess, because I had come in singing "The Wild Colonial Boy."

"Yes, I did win, Adam. Thank you."

The rest of the school year was not as exciting as that first week. Cory and I spent many weekends fishing and hanging out at the docks. Summer came, and I helped Captain Shaw at the docks. One day, Captain Shaw was talking some business with another man who grew cotton. They were making arrangements to take cotton over to England. I don't know why, but I wanted to know why the cotton was taken overseas.

So I asked, "Captain Shaw, sir, what does England do with all this cotton?"

"Why, Ian, they make clothes and linen out of it. Then we buy the clothes and linen from them."

The other man broke in to tell me, "This is a good lesson in economics, son."

"Yes, sir, but why don't we make the clothes and linen here? Wouldn't that be cheaper?"

"Robert, you have to teach this boy about business. He'll never make it with ideas like that. It's not done that way, son."

After that I figured I would stick to sailing. I still did not understand how business worked.

One day, while at the docks, I saw a ship. It was the *Courageous*. I ran over as fast as I could. There on deck were Mr. Moore, Billy, and the rest of the crew. I did not see Old Jim, but I knew he was there.

"Ahoy on board! Request permission to come aboard!"

That was when I saw Old Jim. "Permission granted, Ian Walsh," Old Jim hollered. He remembered my name.

Mr. Moore helped me on board. "Well, fellow, look at you, dressed in fancy clothes. You must have found a gold mine."

"No, sir. It's a long story, though."

"Well, Jack is down below. getting lunch ready. Join us, and you can tell us all about it."

It was funny, but Jack's food had never tasted so good to me before. He was still telling the same stories, but I listened as if I had never heard them. Old Jim finally told Jack to put a knot in his tongue and said to me, "So you are working for Robert Shaw. He's a trader, Mr. Moore."

"Can you blame him, Jim, with what you pay?" Billy answered in my defense.

"Guess not," said Old Jim. "You make sure you mind him, Ian, and you will become a good sailor."

I then proceeded to tell them about Danny. Everyone was quiet.

Mr. Moore asked me to go into city with him. I went with Mr. Moore into the city to show him where to get supplies. They took off that afternoon, and I never saw them again.

~ Growing Up in Charleston ~

In July of 1848, I was invited to go with Cory and his father to Washington DC. We took a carriage part of the way and then caught a train the rest of the trip. On arriving in Washington, Mr. Hendricks gave us a tour. I saw where the president lived and the capitol. The roof was being worked on, because the British had burned it during the War of 1812.

The hotel we checked into was the best in Washington. I had expected that and was starting to settle for nothing less. I think I was becoming a snob, something I had always hated … but for the time being, I enjoyed being on top of the world. The following morning, Mr. Hendricks took us to the capitol with him. He had meetings to attend. Cory and I were to stay around the lobby and wait for him.

The building offered too much for me to see. Cory would have been happy to hang around the lobby, but I convinced him to come exploring with me. I was hoping we might run into President Polk. Cory told me he stayed in the White House most of the time and rarely came over to the capitol. I did not care; I was going to find him if he was in the building. We went up some stairs and entered another floor. We could find no one around. All along the hallway were doors. I opened one after the other. There were rooms behind each door, but nobody was in them. Cory kept trying to stop me. He seemed very nervous. Finally, I opened a door, and there was a huge room with chairs and desks arranged in a semicircle; in the center was a bigger desk and chair. I walked in. The big desk in the middle had a wooden hammer on it.

"Ian, do you know what this place is?"

"No, Cory, but I bet you the president sits in the big chair there with the wooden hammer."

"No, the Speaker of the House does. This is where all the congressmen come to make new laws. See the names of the different states on each of the desks?"

It did not take me long to find South Carolina and sit down in one of the seats. I put my feet up on the desk and got comfortable.

"Ian," Cory hissed, "don't put your feet up on the desk. It belongs to a congressman."

"Wrong, Cory. It belongs to us. The sign plate on the desk says South Carolina, and we are South Carolina. Sit down, Cory."

Just then a tall, slender figure arose from a chair in front of us. Neither Cory nor I had realized that someone else was in the room with us. This very tall man now started to walk toward us. He was dressed all in black.

"Hello," he said, "are you the new congressmen from South Carolina?"

Cory just sat down, put his head down on the desk, and covered it with his hands.

So I answered, "Yes, sir."

"Was it a tough election?"

"We haven't exactly been elected yet."

"Oh, you're just checking the place out, then? Good idea."

"Yes. We will be congressmen someday."

The tall man smiled kindly. "Good. I look forward to seeing you here."

"Sir, how does this place work?" I asked.

"Well, you have a lot of people sitting in those chairs. Each one is given a chance to speak his mind on the issue that is presented. After that, a vote is taken. If there are more yes votes than no votes, it then goes to the Senate or the president. If not, then it dies right here and goes no further."

"So that is how democracy works," I said in awe.

"It is a little more complex than that, but you have a good idea now. Let me ask you this: would you be a slave?"

"No, I would not, sir!"

"Neither would I. So we should not be masters either, then. *That* is democracy."

I understood what he was saying. It sounded so simple the way he expressed it. "Sir, my name is Ian Walsh, and this is my friend Cory Hendricks."

"Cory, are you Tom Hendricks's son?"

Cory raised his head to answer. "Yes, sir. Do you know him?"

"Yes, I do. He is a fine man. We don't always see everything eye-to-eye, but he is an honest and good man. My name, by the way, is Abraham Lincoln. I am a congressman from Illinois. Now tell me, how did you get in here?"

Cory stood up and took charge. "The truth, sir, is that we are lost. We were told to wait in the lobby for my father but started to walk around, and that is how we got here."

Smiling, Mr. Lincoln said, "Follow me. I will take you back to the lobby."

Days seemed to go by so fast for me. The next year came and went. Boots became the perfect duck dog. Grandpa Shaw, Cory, and I became duck hunters. It did not take me long to learn how to shoot a gun.

Before long, 1850 arrived, and in September, Mrs. Shaw gave birth to a baby boy. They named him John, but I called him Jack, and soon everyone else was doing the same. I was fifteen, ready to turn sixteen come December.

One morning I got up early and took Boots to go duck hunting. We went down to the lake. A small, wooden wall had been built near the lake for hunters to hide behind, and that is what I did then. Boots sat right beside me, waiting for his part to come. Not much time passed before some ducks came by. I took aim from behind the wall and fired. I reloaded my gun quickly to take another shot, but the rest of the ducks had vanished.

I said, "Fetch, boy," and off Boots went to retrieve the one duck I had shot.

I ran right behind him, down toward the lake. Not looking where I was going, I tripped over a log near the water. Right by the log, and staring at me, was a coiled up, black, leathery thing. I knew what it was, because Cory had told me about a black snake that was very poisonous. He called it a water moccasin. I was sure it was going to be all over for me, but then Boots came up on the other side of the snake.

The snake changed his attention to Boots, and as he did, I stuck the barrel of my gun onto the coiled-up snake and pulled the trigger, sending the snake flying through the air in several pieces. I hoped that I would never run into another one.

Getting back up to my feet, I looked at Boots, who sat there with his head slanted to one side, as if to say, "What's the matter?"

I just said, "Fetch, boy, and let's go home."

He turned around and picked up the duck. I knew he had no idea that he had just saved my life, but I did. To me, there was no better dog.

The summer I was sixteen, Captain Shaw asked me if I wanted to go to sea on one of his ships. I did not take long to think about it before nodding vigorously. The ship was called the *Philadelphia*, and Captain Shaw said he needed two cabin boys for it. I wondered who the other boy was going to be and asked him.

"It's your roommate, Adam Cooper. I already talked to his father and him about it. Adam is really looking forward to it."

It was not going to be a long trip. The ship was just going up to Boston. Our cargo was cotton. We set sail early in the morning. Adam thought working on the boat was the greatest thing. He was going to become hooked on sailing. I understood that, because it had happened to me.

After two days out at sea, the mainsail was starting to rip. The captain of the ship said it was time to change sails. A sail was brought up from down below. The old one was taken down. As we were putting up the new sail, the halyard got stuck. As hard as the crew tried to free it, it still remained stuck. Everyone got quiet as they looked up at the mast.

The captain said, "Someone is going to have to climb up the mast to see what the problem is. He should be light in weight."

The crew turned their eyes to Adam, who started to step back and try to hide himself. The captain approached him and said, "Well, son, will you do it?"

Adam turned to me for help, but I did not know what to tell him. He walked over to the mast, looked up, and said to the captain, "All right, sir."

Using some rigging, he hoisted himself up. Higher and higher he went. He passed the crow's nest and was not far from the top when I heard him yell, "I found it! I found it!"

He was on his way down and coming fast. When he got to the bottom, he showed the captain a piece of sail. It had wrapped itself around the halyard, causing it to get stuck. The sail went up easily then. Adam became a hero, and we were on our way to Boston again.

The whole trip took about two weeks, and once back in Charleston, I got ready for another school year.

~ The High Seas ~

The next big event in my life came when I finished my schooling at the age of twenty-one. Lisa was more beautiful than ever. Since she had turned sixteen, I had been taking her to dances. She was not that little girl who had chased me around the house anymore.

Captain Shaw set me up as a navigator on one of his ships. I was spending months at sea. The ship I was on finally sailed into Belfast. An eerie feeling overtook me when I stepped off the ship. There was one thing I had to take care of. I took a walk to the cemetery to see that a headstone had been delivered. On it were the words: "Mary Higgins, Beloved Mother and Queen to Danny."

I returned one day to find Mrs. Shaw in hysterics. Captain Shaw and Grandpa had gone to Richmond on business. Mr. Brown, a friend of the family, was at the house, trying to calm her.

Mrs. Shaw said to me, "Ian, it's Jack. He's gotten himself into trouble. The sheriff is out looking for him. I think he'll shoot him if he finds him."

"Now, it can't be that bad. What could Jack have done? He's only seven."

Mr. Brown spoke. "Well, Ian, it seems he's taken his father's carriage for a ride through the city, not exactly staying on the roads."

I didn't need to hear any more to know what had happened. Mrs. Shaw looked at me and said, "Ian, bring my son home to me."

I would hear that request many times. I got a horse from the stable and set out to find him, hopefully before the sheriff. I knew that his horses would be in control and would head home after a while, so I set off to try and cut them off. It was not long before they were heading in my direction. I grabbed hold of the reins and brought the horses to a stop.

"Ian, this is fun!" Jack said.

"Oh, I don't know if Mrs. Johnson will think so. Look what you did to her garden."

"I guess I pulled too hard to the right."

"No, I don't think you pulled hard enough to the left."

"Huh!" My joke went right over his head.

"Forget it, Jack; let's go home."

Captain Shaw finally returned from Richmond. Mrs. Shaw told him about his son and demanded that he have a talk with him. I'll never forget the words he spoke as he looked down at Jack.

He simply said, "Hello, son." Then he went into the study to smoke his pipe.

The time came for me to assume command of my own ship. There was a new addition to the fleet. The ship was called the *Ida Mae* and was built to be one of the fastest ships ever. Captain Shaw gave her to me for her maiden voyage. A British ship had arrived in Charleston, loaded up with cotton and determined to beat us to England to flood the market with its goods. My job would be to see that it failed. I had picked my crew. The first mate was Adam Cooper. Fred Howe was second mate, and he had more than ten years at sea.

When the ship was ready to sail, it was already noon. The British ship had left earlier in the morning. The task seemed impossible, even with a fast ship like the *Ida Mae*. She was on her way, making good time, but there was no sign of the British ship. It was August, so I chose the northern route, which was the shortest. On the eleventh day, a storm hit. I called Adam. Cooper and Mr. Howe to my quarters to see what would be the best way to ride out the storm.

Mr. Howe spoke first. "Captain, may I suggest you pull the sails in and just ride her out?"

"Adam," I said, "how far will this put the ship from England?"

"Sir, we will be pushed south," he replied, "maybe twenty miles out of our way."

"Twenty miles is too many. The captain of the British ship will be bringing his sails in, right?"

Mr. Howe replied, "Yes, sir; it is standard procedure."

"Well, Mr. Howe, take the mainsail down, but leave the jib up to keep us moving and on course. This will be our chance to catch up and overtake them."

The *Ida Mae*, being built for speed, was not a big ship. This would be our best chance. Mr. Howe objected but did as I wished. Adam thought I was crazy, too. He did as I ordered and kept the ship sailing. He called me on deck at one point.

"Sir, the swells are getting too high, and I don't think the bow can take much more of a beating."

"Well, I will get some men; we will bring the anchor around to the stern and drag it behind us. That should stop her from coming crashing down off the swells."

The anchor was brought around to the stern with difficulty, but the problem was solved for now. Luckily, the storm did not get much worse, and two days later, it had vanished.

After seventeen days, we sailed into Liverpool, not knowing if we had beaten the British. The ship was docked and unloaded. We saw no sign of the British ship. The *Ida Mae* had won the race. I gave the crew orders to be back at the ship by five o'clock, so we could set sail; I wanted to get back to Charleston in a hurry. As we were leaving the harbor, the British ship was just arriving. I saluted her captain as we passed each other, and he returned it.

It was late in the day when we arrived back at Charleston. I went out with the crew after we secured the ship. I bought them all a couple of rounds of drinks to thank them. By the time I reached the house, it was already past midnight.

On entering the house, I saw a light on in Captain Shaw's study. I could not see why he would still be up, so I went in. Sitting in the captain's chair was Jack, reading a book and smoking a pipe. He was ten then.

"Jack, why aren't you in bed?"

"Dad and Grandpa went to Richmond, so I am the man of the house now."

"Oh, and what are you reading?"

"*Oedipus Rex.*"

"What? Do you understand it?"

"Sure. It is about this guy who goes out to find his real identity and ends up killing his real father, and then he marries his mother. He didn't realize this, but he made a mess of everything, huh?"

"Yes, I guess he did. He never found what he had started out to 'til it was too late. What about you? Have you found what you're looking for?"

"No!" A puzzled look appeared on his face at this question.

"Well, when you do, I hope it is not too late for you, as it was for Oedipus. How about I relieve you of your duties?"

"Aye, sir. Fishing starts at five in the morning." He handed me the pipe and started to head up to bed.

I called to him. "Jack, next time read a book like *The Last of the Mohicans.*"

He laughed and said to me, "When are you going to marry my sister?"

"Go to bed, Jack."

But he yelled from the stairs, "You're doomed! It is just a matter of time."

He was right. I was doomed; he was going to wake me up at five o'clock in the morning to go fishing.

My race with the British ship would not be the end of my excitement at sea. The next test I faced was my trip to Marseilles, France. We had brought over a cargo of tobacco and were picking up spices, wine, and dresses from Paris. I was to make sure I brought one home for Lisa. A problem occurred on our way home. We were sailing in the Mediterranean Sea when I sighted a ship I had noticed at port. I did not like the looks of the crew and knew they were pirates. They must have set themselves in our path.

There was no way to maneuver the ship to avoid them. The *Ida Mae* could outrun them easily, but I had to get past them first. By then they had fired warning shots from their cannons. The *Ida Mae* had none; she was not built to fight. I called Adam on deck.

"Adam, how many guns do you think they have?" I handed him the looking glass.

"I can only see three, sir."

"That is all I saw, too. My guess is they did not take care of their weapons and are down to just three—all at the bow of the ship, too."

"Yes, but it is enough to blow us apart, Ian."

I thought for a moment, and my gaze fell upon a latrine. This gave me an idea. Kerosene would burn if I could throw it around their cannons. It would surprise them and cause panic among the crew. Now to think of a way to accomplish that ... and then it came to me.

"Not if we disarm them first. Have some men bring up several cases of wine. Empty the wine bottles and then fill them with kerosene from the ship's supply."

"Not the wine, Ian!"

"Yes, I'm afraid so, and you will also need a few dresses. Rip them into rags, soak them in kerosene, and stuff them in the top of the wine bottles. Work fast, Mr. Cooper."

I had Mr. Howe take the mainsail down. The jib had not been put up yet. I then told him to take down the flag and put up a white one. We were going to surrender.

Adam was ready at the stern of the ship with some men. I told him what I wanted him to do when I gave the sign, and I went over to Mr. Howe to give him his next instructions.

"So, Mr. Howe, how fast can you get the sail back up?"

"Very fast," he said. "You'll have it up very fast, sir. Just tell me when."

The pirate ship was very close, approaching toward our stern. The pirates were all on deck, preparing to board the *Ida Mae*. When they were just fifty feet away, I told Adam, who was hiding in the stern with seven other crew members and wine bottles filled with oil, to let them have it. The pirates were mesmerized at first by the flaming wine bottles come flying at them. Before they knew what was happening, their bow was one big flame.

I gave Mr. Howe the order he had been waiting for; up went the mainsail. With one big jolt, the *Ida Mae* was on her way again.

Adam and the rest of the crew were still throwing the wine bottles. The pirates made vain attempts to shoot at us with rifles, but could do nothing as the distance between our two ships grew. The flames kept them away from their cannons, so there was very little they could do to us.

I still had one order left to make. "Mr. Howe, you can take that white rag down and put the flag back up; we will not be surrendering this day."

At home things were getting worse between the South and the North. It was 1860, and Captain Shaw was spending much of his time in Richmond and at the South Carolina capitol building in Columbia. I met with him to discuss some business in England that he wanted me to handle personally. Once again I was at sea. I spent almost five months in England finishing what I had to do.

On April 11, 1861, the *Ida Mae* pulled into Charleston Harbor. As the ship passed Fort Sumter, I gave a salute to Major Robert Anderson as he stood on the huge walls of the fort. He had a worried look on his face and looked puzzled that there was no flag on my ship. There were many reasons for that, but it didn't seem to matter right then.

Captain Shaw was waiting for me at the docks and hurried me back to the house. I knew that on December 20, 1860, South Carolina had voted to secede from the Union.

"Ian, things are getting worse. I don't see any way to avoid a war with the North anymore. The North will not give up the fort, so it looks as if we will have to use force to take her."

This explained why I had seen so many soldiers in Charleston. Early the next morning, I was awakened by the sounds of thunder.

It was only 4:30 a.m., but I knew what the sound was and headed down to the docks.

The Confederacy had opened fire on Fort Sumter. There was no way out of war now.

I noticed a young lieutenant standing by the water, watching and rubbing his jaw. It was Cory Hendricks. I went over to talk to him.

"You are still trying to make me feel miserable about your chin?"

"Dang it, Ian Walsh, it has never been the same—it keeps going out on me. But how are you doing? Been away for a long time?"

"Aye, and I see a lot has happened here."

"Yes, but it should all be over in a few months. That's how long it should take us to march into Washington and set Old Abe right."

"I hope you are right," I told him. "You know, it may not be that easy."

"You wait and see. This is different."

I left him to return home. I never saw him again. He never made it past the first battle at a place called Manassas. He had been right. It was different, and a very short war for him.

I spent a lot of time at the spot on the lake that he had first taken me to. It was still quiet as ever, and I was the only one who knew it existed now.

I never joined up, even though everyone was expecting me to. It wasn't long before I was one of only a few men still left in Charleston. I came up with an idea for Captain Shaw to try to run through the blockade the federal Navy was putting around Charleston. He told me that my plan sounded good, but Jeff Davis had decided to stop all shipments of cotton to Europe in order to put pressure on them to aid us.

"But," I said, "they will just use wool and stay out of the war anyhow."

"I know that, Ian, but I can't go against my country."

I understood the position he was in and let it die. His ships would spend the war tied up at the docks.

~ The Coward ~

In 1863, the war was still on. I was being labeled a coward. Even Captain Shaw had thought I would sign up. He never said anything to me, but I felt I was letting him down. He would have joined himself, but he had fallen at the docks, breaking his leg in two places. He could barely walk. The doctor told him that his leg would never be the same.

Lisa was the most important reason that I never did join. She did everything she could to stop me every time I came close to joining. She could not only talk me into something, but also out of it. One evening Lisa and I were walking by the docks when some soldiers, who had just come out of a pub, started whistling at Lisa and making comments to me.

I held myself together all right until one of them said, "Hey, honey, why don't you come with us and leave that useless coward?"

I was not going to stand by and be called a coward; my hands were in fists, and I was moving toward them.

Lisa grabbed my arm tightly and said, "Ian, don't. I am not going to stand here and watch you fight."

I said, "Close your eyes, then. It will only take a second."

Her grip became tighter, and she said, "Take me home now!" So I did.

Jack, on the other hand, was a different story. He was all ready to join in the fight. The only thing that stopped him was that he was only twelve and had not figured out a way to enlist yet.

His mother asked me to have a talk with him, but every time I tried, the reply was always the same: "You're a coward, and I'm not listening to a coward."

This hurt me a great deal. I couldn't care less what the others said, but Jack was different. Maybe he was speaking the truth.

June came, and Jack found a way to enlist. I came down for breakfast to find Mrs. Shaw in tears. Captain Shaw looked so old sitting in the chair. He said to me, "Jack left a note in his room. He volunteered with a South Carolina regiment. My father went down to see if he could stop him."

At that moment, Grandpa Shaw returned. "I was too late. They have already left for Virginia."

In a choked voice, Mrs. Shaw pleaded, "Ian, bring my son home to me."

I headed to the door, and Captain Shaw spoke up. "Take Joey with you." Joey was the Captain's prize horse and his fastest.

"Thank you, sir." It was the first time I saw a tear fall from his eye.

I knew of only one way to get to Jack. I headed for my old school, where Jack would have been starting in September. Mr.

Dodd was still there and was in charge of recruiting. "Ian, come in. I'm surprised to see you. How can I help you?"

"I'm looking for a kid," I explained. "He is twelve years old and has on fancy boots, and he talks too much, too."

He looked down at my boots. "Are the boots like the ones you have on?"

"Yes, we shop at the same stores in London."

"He was here—set out with the rest of them this morning, I signed him up as a musician. There is one other thing, too. He has the strangest name: Oedipus Rex."

"Can I join that regiment?"

"Yes, they need an officer. I was going to let General Lee assign one when they arrived in Richmond. I will notify him I am sending someone for the job." Mr. Dodd handed me my orders. I held the rank of captain. I guess I more than qualified for the position. A few things still remained to be done before I left for Richmond. Mr. Dodd had given me a sword, but all I had for a uniform was a pair of dark gray pants and a bluish gray shirt with red flowers printed on it. The only hat I had was a white straw one. I had six days before I had to head out.

Next I went to see Mr. Shaw. I found him at home in his study. I knocked lightly on the door before entering.

"Come in," he answered. He was just sitting in his chair, staring out the window; he seemed in a daze.

"It's Ian, sir. I wanted to talk to you."

"Of course, Ian. What is it?"

I was nervous and was having a hard time trying to find the words. So it just came out.

"Sir, I would like your permission to ask your daughter for her hand in marriage." I had finally said it.

He got up out of his chair, looked out the window, and then turned to me.

"Yes, Ian. You have my permission."

I didn't know what I was going to say next.

"Well, Ian, just don't stand there—there's a lot to do."

"Oh, yes, sir."

I didn't know what to do next, so Mr. Shaw said, "Son, you have to go to downtown Charleston and get a ring."

"A ring … yes, sir."

"Mrs. Shaw and I will take care of everything else. Don't forget to ask Lisa for her hand in marriage. Now get going—there are a lot of preparations to be done."

I left after telling Mr. Shaw to have Lisa meet me down by the docks at five.

Downtown, I found a jewelry store and picked out a set of rings. It was close to five now, so I hurried to meet Lisa at the docks. She was there waiting for me. Behind her I saw the fort with the stars and bars flying over it. I came up behind her and caught her by surprise.

"Darn you, Ian! What's so important that you wanted to meet me here?"

"Follow me to the *Ida Mae*, and I'll show you." We went to over to where the *Ida Mae* was on the docks; it was empty now. We then walked up the plank and onto the ship. I took her up to the bow of the ship and asked her to look out over the water.

"This is where I spend most of my time writing. Isn't it beautiful?"

"Yes, Ian, but why did you bring me up here?" I went down on one knee and held both her hands. "To ask you for your hand in marriage," I said, and then I pulled out the ring and put it on her finger.

"Yes, Ian! I will, I will!"

I got up, gave her a hug, and said, "We have to get to the church."

"The church?" she repeated with a puzzled look.

"Yes. Why wait? Your father and mother arranged everything." She smiled, gleaming with joy. We ran all the way to the church.

The Shaws had everything ready. It was grand; the church was decorated beautifully and filled with people. Jack was the only one missing. After the wedding, Lisa and I went to an inn in downtown Charleston. After we checked in, I picked her up and carried her up to our room.

The following morning, we got up, had breakfast, and then went for a walk. She was curious as to why Jack had not been at our ceremony the night before, and I told her. I then told her I had enlisted. This did not go over too well, and she ran off. I returned to the Shaw residence in hope that she would show up there. She did, and I was glad, because I could not leave her like this.

"Ian, I can't let you go like this." She came running over to me as I was getting Joey ready for the journey. She fell into my arms.

"Lisa, I'm sorry I didn't tell you sooner, but it is time for me—I have no choice now. I'm doing it for you, for the future we are going to have together, and for Jack. I'm tired of what is being done to our city: empty warehouses, people starving because there is not enough food to go around, the blockade, and constant shelling from the sea."

"I know, Ian. My father explained a lot to me."

"I'll return when it's all over."

"God be with you, Ian." I gave her a kiss good-bye, climbed on Joey, and rode off.

I reached the regiment late in the evening; it was after ten. They had been expecting me. The sergeant greeted me. "Welcome, Captain Walsh. The men will be ready for you to inspect tomorrow morning, if you wish."

"Yes, that will be fine, Sergeant," I told him. "What is going on by that campfire?"

"The men are just letting off some steam—playing cards and gambling."

"I think I will join them."

I knew Jack would be there. I walked up behind him. All the other soldiers saw me and dropped their cards with blank looks on their faces. Jack still didn't see me and, with a cigar in his mouth, reached forward to grab the money.

Speaking out of the corner of his mouth, he said, "Guess I'm too good for you all."

Before he could get the money, I lifted him up off the log he was sitting on.

"Hey, put me down!" Jack cried out as he turned to see who it was. His cigar dropped from his mouth, and he became speechless when he saw that it was me.

"Who is this?" I asked.

"Why, he is our musician, sir," the soldiers all answered at once.

"Oh! Well, Sergeant, from now on, all musicians will be bedded down by nine. Otherwise, they might lose their rhythm. Lack of sleep can do that."

"Yes, sir," the sergeant answered.

I started to escort Jack to his tent. "What about my money? It is still over there!" Jack started to holler.

I told him, "Guess you have made a donation."

"To who?"

"That is 'to *whom*,' and it is to the Catholic Church."

"But I'm Protestant," he argued.

"Looks as if you've just received a vision."

"What vision?"

"The one that shows me belt tanning your butt if I ever catch you gambling or smoking again," I explained.

He was quiet again. I broke the silence to ask him which was his tent. He lifted his finger up and pointed to one. We went over to it, and Jack climbed in.

As I started to leave, he called to me, "Ian, I'm sorry. You're not a coward."

"Go to sleep, Oedipus Rex."

"Ian, it would have been better for Oedipus to have stayed with his adopted parents. They loved him."

"Jack," I told him, "You may be closer to what you are looking for than you realize … and Jack, did I tell you? You are my brother-in-law now."

"You married my sister! I knew it!" he shouted out and let out the biggest rebel yell I had ever heard. Shouts came from the other tents. The whole camp now knew.

The next morning, the regiment moved out. These men looked nothing like the First New York, but they had a spirit in them that I had never seen before. I turned to Jack, who was at the end of the column.

"Give us some music, Master Shaw."

He started to play his drum and sing: "Sitting by the roadside on a summer's day, chattin' with my mess mates and passin' time away. Hidin' in the shadow underneath the trees. Goodness how delicious, eatin' goober peas."

I thought I was going to regret letting Jack pick the song, but I soon saw my way out when Jack let me cut in with the next verse: "I think that this song has lasted almost long enough. Yeah, the subject's interestin', but the rhymes are mighty rough. I wish this war were over, when free from rags and thieves, we'd kiss our wives and sweethearts and gobble goober peas."

The next song was my favorite, "Hallowed Ground." I had the men march all day. The orders I received said we were going north to Harrisburg. The idea was to threaten Washington and bring the war to the North.

We camped just outside of Richmond. I had meetings with my superiors most of the day. The following morning, we would make the march toward Pennsylvania. All the men were lined up and ready to move out.

That was when I noticed something strange on Jack's shirt. Between his top two buttons was a black thread that seemed to wiggle and then vanish. I moved closer and bent down to see what it was. This thread had a green head behind it, with black eyes staring right at me. I didn't know what to say and stayed there looking at it in amazement.

Jack finally said, "He's a garter snake. I found him this morning."

"Oh!" I said. "He isn't coming with us, is he?"

"Do you think I should leave him here?"

"Most definitely. He has no legs for marching, and everyone must march on his own."

"I didn't think of that, sir."

And with that, he let the snake go in the grass, where it promptly disappeared.

The men endured four more days of marching before I received word to move out and make haste to a place called Gettysburg.

We finally arrived at Gettysburg in the late afternoon. I went to check out the lay of the land as soon as camp was set up. I returned back in time for dinner. After dinner I found a tree to sit under and do some writing in my diary.

"Captain, it is almost three in the morning. Aren't you going to get some sleep?"

"Aye, Sergeant. I guess I dozed off. I was thinking about an old friend. I haven't seen him in a long time."

"Don't worry, sir, you'll see him again, sooner than you think. Why, just tonight I ran into my cousin from Tennessee. Last time I saw him, we were just youngsters growing up on our farm in South Carolina. He and his family moved to Tennessee—haven't seen him 'til now. Just think: it took a war to bring us together."

"War is funny that way, Sergeant. Maybe there will be a time when we won't need a war to bring us together."

"That would be nice, sir, but I can't see it."

"There is always hope." I yawned and said, "I will turn in in just a minute, Sergeant."

"Yes, sir. I will be up for a while if you need anything."

"And, Sergeant, have our musician report to me after breakfast tomorrow morning."

"Yes, sir. I'll see to it."

The sergeant left. There had already been two days of fighting, and my regiment had arrived late. I was used to missing the action, but the next day, July 3, would make up for those two days.

The morning came too soon for me. I ate some fried pork and bread in my tent and then took out my pen to write some letters and fill out some paperwork. I heard a knock at the tent's entrance and bid whoever it was to come inside. It was Jack.

"Private Jack Shaw reports as ordered, sir."

"Good. At ease, soldier. I want you to take these papers to General Lee. You are to hand them to him personally. Is that understood?"

"Yes, sir, but aren't we going to split the Yankees in two today?"

"We? No, you have your orders," I told him, "and I am counting on you."

"I won't let you down, Ian."

"I know you won't. And Jack ... I want you to hold this for me."

"It is your diary. You should keep it."

"You can give it to me later."

"I will take good care of it. I am off to complete my top-secret mission for the Confederacy." He saluted me and left the tent.

The only thing left to do was have the men line up in battle formation. I called to the sergeant. "It is time. Get the men ready."

It took only seconds for the men to get in line; they had been waiting for this day. We moved into the open field. Cannonballs were landing all around us, but the men did not flinch, instead standing ready. I looked back at the trees. Standing there beneath one of them was a boy dressed in the uniform of the First New York. He had a drum, and he looked up at me and smiled as he started to play. It was Danny. I remembered what Danny had said: everything would be all right.

I took my sword out and raised it up to the sky. Looking back again, I saw that no one stood under the tree now. I saw General George Pickett. I waited for his nod. It came. I brought my sword down ninety degrees and moved forward with thirty men following.

As we moved across the open field, the shelling became more intense. Despite this, our formation stayed together. It was such an amazing thing to see a wall of men, stretching more than a mile long, moving together. The Yankees kept blasting us. The men moved on, but gaps began to appear in the line as whole regiments seemed to vanish. The screams of wounded men became so loud they could be heard over all the gunfire.

I reached a fence and turned around to give the order to climb over it, but only found four men still with me, and the battlefield around me was in complete chaos. Climbing on top of the fence and putting my hat on the tip of my sword, I started waving it and yelling for the men to rally. They must have seen me, because the next thing I knew, they were trying to get back into formation. Men were running toward me from everywhere.

Suddenly, the blast of a nearby explosion threw me off the fence. A soldier helped me to my feet.

"Are you all right, sir?" he inquired in a tenuous voice.

He was scared, and so was I. A warm feeling ran down the left side of my face, but I ignored it.

"Form on the other side of the fence!" I shouted out.

The men did as I ordered, and I led them forward again. Our target was a clump of trees on the far side of the battlefield. My uniform became drenched with blood from the wound to my head. I was hit again—this time by a Minnie ball to my left shoulder—but I stayed up and continued to head for the trees. The men were still behind me. We were close enough to see the Yanks, and I ordered a volley to be unloaded on them. It was time for a bayonet charge. We ran right at that clump of trees. The Yanks tried to hold their ground but soon took to flight in the face of our charge.

Feeling very weak, I leaned against a tree in the brief lull, but when I looked up again, I saw a wall of blue uniforms headed right at me. The Yanks were returning, and I ordered the men to fire on them. There were so many of them that I could see we were going to be overrun, and no help was on the way.

Whoever was left with me put up a fight as the close combat became hand-to-hand, but we were outnumbered; the fight lasted only seconds. I collapsed.

Looking up, I saw a Yankee general forming his men for an attack. In front of them I saw a cannon and boxes of ammunition. Grabbing a rifle from a dead soldier and seeing that it was loaded, I got to my knees and with my one good arm, I pointed the rifle and fired at the boxes. I hit them! They exploded, and a big flame shot into the air. The Yanks broke formation and took cover. The Yankee general got up off the ground and saw me still kneeling across the field. He had the most astonished look on his face. He took his revolver out of the holster and pointed it at me, but I collapsed.

When I opened my eyes again, that Yankee general was kneeling beside me. "Easy, Captain. You're hurt pretty bad," he said in a familiar voice. "The orderlies will be here soon."

I looked into his eyes and smiled. "Lieutenant Michael Smith, I surrender."

"Ian, is that you?" he asked.

"Yes, sir," I said weakly.

"Orderlies, orderlies over here!" he shouted.

"It's too late, sir."

"Don't talk, Ian." He tried to comfort me.

"Sir, I need you to do something for me. Captain Robert Shaw in Charleston has a son; his name is Jack. I want you to tell him what happened to me. He needs to know. Promise me you will do that."

"I will," he said. "You have my word on that. I will tell him that he can be very proud of you."

"Tell him I'm no coward."

"I will," he said.

"Sir, I am sorry about that explosion."

"I know you are, and I forgive you, even if you ruined my countercharge."

"I guess we are even now," I told him.

"How is that?" He looked puzzled.

"You drank my milk."

We both started laughing, but the pain got to be too much for me, and I had to stop.

"Keep still, Ian. No more jokes," my old commander said soothingly.

"It's all right, sir. Jack has my diary, and he will be able to finish it … I hear Danny playing his drum. Do you hear it?"

Michael Smith shook his head sadly.

"It's all right, sir; I can hear it. I can go to sleep now."

~ Epilogue: Jack Shaw ~

General Smith kept his promise to Ian. It was several months after the war ended that a lone Yankee walked up to our house. My father went outside and met him first. Then he called for me to come outside, and my father introduced me to the Yankee. I saw from the uniform that he was an officer—a general.

"Hello, Master Shaw. I'm General Michael Smith. I was a friend of Ian's," he said to me. Then he invited me to go for a walk with him. He told me everything that had happened that day in July 1863.

As for what happened to me that day, I had followed my instructions and ran all the way to General Robert E. Lee's headquarters. I went to his tent to give him the papers but was stopped. Two soldiers grabbed me and would not let me go.

"I have to see the general!" I told them. "Let me go! I have to hand him these papers."

"Get lost, kid."

Just then, the general stepped out of his tent and said, "What is all this commotion out here?"

"Sorry, sir. It is this kid; he won't leave."

The general looked at me. "Son, what seems to be the trouble?"

"Sir, Private Jack Shaw reports. I have these papers for you from Captain Ian Walsh of South Carolina."

"At ease, son, and come into my tent. The name of your captain sounds familiar."

Inside the tent, the general took the papers from me. I saw him reading them, and he asked me, "Have you read these papers, son?"

"No," I answered.

He went to his desk, and I could hear him muttering, "What have I done? It's my fault; it's all my fault." He picked up his pen from his desk, signed one of the papers, and then stamped it. As he handed the papers back to me, he said, "I am sorry, it's my fault," and kept muttering those same words over and over as he left the tent.

I opened up one of the documents to read it. It was a personal letter to General Lee.

Dear Sir,

A long time ago, in Mexico, you told me a story and said that I should face my scorpion next time I meet him. Today I have gone out to do that. The boy standing in front of you will face many scorpions in his lifetime, but right now, he needs his mother. I'm asking you to sign his discharge

papers and final orders to send him home, where
he belongs.

Captain Ian Walsh
South Carolina

The next paper held my discharge from the Army of Northern
Virginia, signed and stamped with the seal of the Confederacy,
and on the last paper were my final orders:

Private Jack Shaw,
Your last assignment is to go home to your mother
and father, where you belong. It will be up to you
now to look after your sister. You will have to
finish my diary for me, and when the time comes,
you will know what to do with it.

Captain Ian Walsh
South Carolina

I ran out of the tent to see soldiers running and stumbling
all over the place. I grabbed a soldier as he ran by me, knocking
him to the ground. I leaned down, held on tight to his shirt, and
looked into his eyes.

"Where are the men from South Carolina? Where are they?"
I yelled.

His eyes had already told me the answer. He had been
someplace that was not meant for man.

He said to me, "Gone, gone, all of them gone. They're gone!"

Tears started to run down his face. I had never seen a grown man cry before. I released his shirt and stood up.

An officer came over to me and threw a gun into my hand. "The Yankees may countercharge. Be ready," he said.

They never did, though. I will never know why.

Late that afternoon, the march south had started. I marched without my drum and without a regiment. Silence seemed to cover the road, even though it was filled with men. I don't know why, but the words to "Hallowed Ground" started to sound from my mouth, and soon everyone was singing it.

I am not sure exactly, but it must have taken three, maybe four days for me to reach Richmond, Virginia. Once there I went to the train station. Asking around, I found a train that would take me to Charleston.

I went to board the train, but a man stepped in front of me and said, "Where do you think you're going, kid?"

Pulling out my paper with General Lee's signature and the stamp of the Confederacy on it, I replied, "Step aside. I am on official business."

He moved without saying a word, and I boarded the train, found a seat, and collapsed into it. A woman with a little girl sat across from me. The little girl was staring at me, and I noticed a spot of blood on the shirt of my uniform. So that was what she was looking at. She went into her mother's basket, pulled out a biscuit, and held it out for me to take. I looked at the woman, who nodded for me to go ahead. I was starved, and I ate it in two seconds. Then another one came out of the basket. By the time I was finished, I had eaten six biscuits. If there had been more, I would have eaten them, too. It occurred to me then that the biscuits had been meant for someone else, but he was probably someplace far away now, and would have no use for biscuits.

Sleep must have overtaken me then, because the next thing I knew was that I was in Wilmington, North Carolina. From there, it was Florence, South Carolina. I fell asleep again. Days must have passed. A gentle touch on my knee woke me up. "This is Charleston; it is the last stop." It was the lady across from me; her voice sounded so sweet that I smiled for the first time since leaving Gettysburg.

I left the station and walked along the docks. My father's ships were still there. I soon made the turnoff at Ashley and onto Calhoun, toward my house. The gates were open. I saw Boots on the front porch. He did not bark, but looked at me and whimpered. He knew.

I walked into the house. There was no one in sight. Hearing a noise from the kitchen, I headed in that direction. Stopping at the entrance to it, I saw my mother skinning yams. I could tell she had been crying. Thanks to the invention of a thing called the telegraph, the news of Gettysburg had reached Charleston long before I did.

I stood at the doorway and watched her. She must have sensed it, because she dropped her knife and turned around. I ran into her arms, burying my face in her dress, and cried. My father soon appeared with Grandpa and my sister.

Tears shined in my father's eyes as he came over and gave me a hug. "Welcome home, son. Welcome home."

The war raged on for another two years. Grandpa took it the hardest. He had started the Shaw's mighty shipping empire and was about to see it all lost with the defeat of the South.

I don't think my sister ever got over the loss of Ian. She made herself busy, I think, to take her mind off of it. We never forgot Ian; he had left a part of himself with our family. It seemed I was always being reminded of this.

The military academy was now housing for federal troops. The Yankees were taking over everything. My father woke me one morning and told me to get dressed; we had to get to the docks fast. I was fourteen.

Down at the docks, Grandpa was standing on the deck of the *Savannah* when I arrived. I recognized another ship. It was the *Philadelphia.* She had gone to sea with the *Ida Mae,* but had never returned. The ship's captain was Adam Cooper, and the Union Jack was flying over her. I could not figure that out.

Federal troops were headed in our direction. On reaching us, a young captain approached my father and asked, "Sir, are you Captain Robert Shaw?"

"Yes, I am," answered my father.

"Well, sir, I have orders to seize your ships as part of war reparations."

"I do not think you can do that, Captain," my father replied.

Just then I saw the most wonderful thing take place. Starting with the *Ida Mae,* the Union Jack went up. Then the same thing happened on board the *Delaware,* the *New Jersey,* the *King David,* the *Crusader,* and, lastly, the *Savannah.* They were all flying the Union Jack now.

From the deck of the *Savannah,* Grandpa was yelling at the Yankees. "Stay off of the Queen's ships, you bloodsucking vermin." He started to dance and sing. The song he chose was "God Save the Queen." He was still the Grandpa I remembered.

My father tried to explain to the captain that the ships belonged to the Queen of England now, and he had no authority to turn them over to anyone.

The captain replied, "Sir, if this is a trick of yours, it won't work. I have my orders. I will ask you kindly to move aside."

Adam now stepped in. "Captain, these ships belong to the British Crown, and if you attempt to board them or interfere with them sailing, I will notify the British ambassador in Washington at once. They were registered in February of 1861 with the British government."

The captain looked baffled. He finally sent a messenger to find out from headquarters what to do. The messenger returned with the answer: hands off Her Majesty's ships—something about not wanting to cause a diplomatic incident. The captain withdrew his men from the docks and never bothered us again.

Adam explained everything to me. My father and Ian had decided not to take any chances with his ships and money. On Ian's last trip, he had taken much of my father's money and placed it in an English bank. Then he had registered all of my father's ships with the British Commerce Department. Adam had since added three more ships to my father's fleet and set up an office in Liverpool. My father was now the owner of one of the fastest growing British shipping companies. As Ian would have said, it was a grand day for the Shaw Family.

I am now twenty-five, and as captain of the *Ida Mae*, I have sailed all over the world. Once in a while, I get back to Charleston to see my family. This morning, home for the holidays, I awoke with the realization that Ian's diary was just about complete, and I knew what he had meant when he said I would know what to do with it when the time came.

A knocking sound came from outside my room. "Who is there?" I asked.

"It is Timmy, Uncle Jack. Mom wants to know if you are coming down for breakfast."

"Tell your mother yes, but come in first. I have something to give you."

Timmy is Ian's son, and the diary was meant for him.

"What is it, Uncle Jack?"

"How old are you now, Timmy?"

"I'm twelve, sir."

I handed him a worn, leather-bound volume. "This is your father's diary. I think you are old enough to have it now."

He took the book, looked at it, opened it up, and started to read. I could see the tears forming in his eyes, despite his best effort to hold them back. He finally said, "Thank you, sir. I will tell Mom you will be down soon for breakfast."

"Good, and how about after breakfast, we go get the biggest Christmas tree in all of Charleston?"

"Yes, sir, the biggest in all America," he called as he headed toward the door.

"Timmy, what is for breakfast?" I shouted.

The corners of his mouth went up, and a bright smile appeared. The answer came without hesitation: "Goober peas, Oedipus Rex!"